The Father's Embrace

An Encounter with Divine Mercy

The Father's Embrace
An Encounter with Divine Mercy

Rev. Fr. Gregory E. Ogbenika, Ph.D.

Elisheba House
Trinity, FL, USA

Nihil Obstat:

Rev. Fr. Gregory Obanado, Ph.D.
Parish Priest,
St. Anthony Catholic Church
Iraokhor, Edo State, Nigeria

And Lecturer,
Seminary of All Saints, Uhiele-Ekpoma,
Edo State, Nigeria

Imprimatur.

Most Rev. Dr. Gabriel G.G. Dunia
Bishop
Catholic Diocese of Auchi,
Auchi, Edo State Nigeria
August 8, 2018

Copyright © 2018 Gregory E. Ogbenika, PhD.
All Rights Reserved

No part of this publication may be reproduced, stored in a retrieval system or transmitted in any form, by any means, electronic, mechanical, photocopy, recording, or otherwise, without the prior permission of the copyright owner.

Published by:

Elisheba House
Trinity, Fl, USA
www.elishebahouse.com

ISBN-13: 978-1732137721
ISBN-10: 1732137722

DEDICATION

This work is dedicated to those who are committed to spreading the message of Divine Mercy.

ACKNOWLEDGMENTS

I would like to thank the Almighty God for his abiding presence in my life and in my ministry as his priest. This is evident in the so many ways he has manifested his magnanimity and mercy upon me, as I follow him on the path of service in his vineyard to enhance the sanctification and salvation of my brothers and sisters in the Lord. Profound thanks to the Almighty God for his guidance and wisdom from above that influenced and saw to the completion of this book. May His holy name be glorified both now and forever. Amen

Special thanks to the Holy Father, Pope Francis for bringing to the fore once again the need to be merciful as the Father is merciful, especially during the Extra Ordinary Jubilee Year of Mercy. Profound thanks to my Bishop, Most Rev. G.G. Dunia, for his usual paternal guidance and for giving approval for this book to be published.

It is always a thing of Joy to have students who are thoughtful and challenging, when engaged in any academic exercise. It is on that note that I would like to express my gratitude to Leo Luka and Clement Ajibolade for their insight and critique of this noble enterprise.

Furthermore, I was helped to broaden the horizon of this work by communicating my thoughts and insight on an issue as important as Divine Mercy to a group of committed Catholics, who were ready to continue to advance in their knowledge of the faith during the summer class of 2016 at St. Ignatius of Antioch Catholic Church, Tarpon Springs, Florida. This was awakened through questions, comments, observations and criticisms. I give kudos to those who were in that summer class for encouraging me to publish this work.

My profound thanks to Msgr. Joseph Pellegrino, Pastor of St. Ignatius Catholic Church, for allowing this class to take place and for providing the enabling environment for these thoughts to blossom. Special thanks to the following people for their immense contributions to the realization of this work: Ivonne and Rick Hernandez, the Women's Council at St. Ignatius of Antioch Catholic Church, Tarpon Springs, Fl, Laurann Schmitt, and John and Barbara Donnell to mention but a few.

I render unalloyed appreciation to all who work to spread the message of Divine Mercy throughout the whole world. May we all obtain mercy in return for mercy from the most merciful God now and always. Amen

FOREWORD

Since the pontificate of St. John Paul II, the Church has been enriched by a greater understanding of the Mercy of God. St. John Paul II promoted this devotion, developed the revelations of St. Faustina Kowalska, and gave the Church Divine Mercy Sunday, the Sunday after Easter. During the canonization liturgy for St. Faustina, St. John Paul II said, "This consoling message is addressed above all to those who, afflicted by a particularly harsh trial or crushed by the weight of the sins they committed, have lost all confidence in life and are tempted to give into despair. To them the gentle face of Christ is offered; those rays from His heart touch them and shine upon them, warm them, show them the way and fill them with hope. How many souls have been consoled by the prayer 'Jesus, I trust in you', which Providence initiated through St. Faustina! This simple act of abandonment to Jesus dispels the thickest clouds and lets a ray of light penetrate every life."

Pope Francis has spent much of his papacy developing the wonder of God's Mercy. He provided the Church with a Jubilee Year of Mercy. After opening the Holy Door at the Basilica of St. Mary Major, Pope Francis said, "God's ability to forgive knows no limits as His mercy frees people from bitterness and despair. The church's forgiveness must be every bit as broad as that offered by Jesus on the Cross and by Mary at His feet. There is no other way." Pope Francis speaks often of the unlimited bounds of the Mercy of God. He often adds that the only limit there is on God's mercy is the limit that we put on His mercy by presuming that we are beyond His mercy and thus refusing to seek and even refusing to accept His gift of mercy.

It would be easy for us to focus on the Mercy of God as a gift we have received. But there is much more to be considered. The Mercy of God is the way that we can make His love real in the world. By extending His mercy to others, they can have an experience of the Loving Father.

How is it that we can do this? How can we be merciful as our Father is Merciful? (Luke 6:36) In *The Father's Embrace: An Encounter with Divine Mercy,* Fr. Gregory Ogbenika has provided us with a succinct guide for rendering God's Mercy real in the world. He does this by re-examining the Spiritual Works of Mercy and the Corporal Works of Mercy. He considers each gift in detail and presents practical ways that we can exercise each gift. Fr. Ogbenika does not shrink from calling us to exhibit those gifts that for most are quite difficult. For example, he calls us to be merciful to the sinner by admonishing him as a brother. He calls us to bear wrongs patiently as a distinctive feature of the mercy of the crucified Jesus. Nor does Fr. Ogbenika gloss over the responsibility we have to reach out to others in need. In his introduction to the section on the Corporal Works of Mercy, Fr. Ogbenika quotes Karl Rahner, *"God's mercies to a man always compel him in turn to show mercy. Mercy sees the distress of others as his own."*

"From everyone to whom much has been given, much will be required (Luke 12:48)." We have received an abundance of mercy. We need to give an abundance of mercy. Fr. Ogbenika guides us in the establishment of God's Kingdom on earth by showing us how to become living witnesses and examples of Divine Mercy.

Rev. Msgr. Joseph A. Pellegrino
Pastor, St. Ignatius of Antioch Catholic Church
Tarpon Springs, FL, USA

TABLE OF CONTENTS

DEDICATION V

ACKNOWLEDGMENTS VII

FOREWORD IX

INTRODUCTION 1

CHAPTER ONE

DIVINE MERCY IN THE HOLY BIBLE AND SOME FATHERS OF THE CHURCH 5

    Divine Mercy in the Old Testament 6
    Divine Mercy and compassion in the New Testament 9
        The Gospels 9
        St. Paul on Divine Mercy 10
    Church Fathers on the Mercy of God 13
        St. Thomas Aquinas 13
        St. Pope John Paul II 13
        Pope Francis 14
        A Summary of the Papal Bull "Misericordiae Vultus" by which Pope Francis Convoked the Extra Ordinary Jubilee Year of Mercy 15
    Conclusion 21

CHAPTER TWO

SPIRITUAL WORKS OF MERCY 23

Introduction..23
    1. Counselling the Doubtful...24
    2. Admonishing the Sinner 25
    3. Instructing the Ignorant 28
    4. Comforting the Sorrowful 30
    5. Bearing Wrongs Patiently...31
    6. Forgiving Injuries 33
    7. Praying for the Living and the Dead 35
Conclusion 37

CHAPTER THREE

CORPORAL WORKS OF MERCY..39

Introduction..39
    1. Feed the Hungry 42
    2. Give drink to the thirsty 46
    3. Bury the Dead...50
    4. Visit the Sick 54
    5. Clothe the Naked..56
    6. Habour the Homeless..60
    7. Comfort the Prisoner..62
Conclusion 64

CHAPTER FOUR

THE NEED FOR RECONCILIATION WITH GOD AND NEIGHBOUR IN THE LIGHT OF THE EXTRA ORDINARY JUBILEE YEAR OF MERCY 67

   Introduction 67
   What is Reconciliation? 69
   Reconciliation with God 71
   Reconciliation with our Neighbour 73
   Reconciliation within the Context of the Extraordinary Jubilee Year of Mercy 77
   Conclusion 82

FINAL THOUGHTS 85

SELECTED BIBLIOGRAPHY 89

INTRODUCTION

Without prejudice to so many other considerations on Divine Mercy, it is above all, the completion of what is lacking. Mercy is therefore the instrument by which what is deficient is made whole. It completes and complements. To have mercy on somebody or something is to add up and bring to fruition, that which is apart from this realization. To this effect, Rev. Kosicki says: "to be merciful... is to love them and ask the Father of Mercies to bless them with his presence."[1] "Etymologically, the word mercy can be traced to the Latin root; *Miserere*. From this we have *miser*, which relates to poverty. Mercy in this light is the act of enriching.

St. Thomas Aquinas says that when love meets misery, mercy is born.[2] Mercy can be bestowed or obtained by anyone at any time. This is because, no one is an island. Sometimes, we stand in need of one thing or the other or even our fellow human beings. Sometimes, we ourselves are also needed. This need is achievable mostly in the care we give.

Care for ourselves, neighbour and environment is an integral requirement for the authentic existence of man. In the recent times, this fact is so evident. The reason is that

---

[1] George W. Kosicki, *I Demand Deeds of Mercy*, Mumbai: St. Paul Publications, 2000, p. 34.
[2] St. Thomas Aquinas, *Summa Theologica* 2a, 2ae 30.

most of the troubles in our world today are caused by lack of care. When we fail to care for water and aquatic creatures, we face the problem of flooding and the loss of aquatic creatures like fish and remain in want. We experience excessive sunshine, because we have destroyed the ozone layer. These and many others cut short our life span and make this world inhabitable. To resolve this tension, we need mercy. Thus, the Holy Father, Pope Francis, in his encyclical, *Laudato Si*, says that "the urgent challenge to protect our common home includes a concern to bring the whole human family together to seek a sustainable and integral development... The Creator does not abandon us; he never forsakes his loving plan or repents of having created us. Humanity still has the ability to work together in building our common home."[3]

Man's mercy is analogous to Divine Mercy. In this vein, we need the Divine Mercy to make our understanding and conception of mercy clear and authentic. It means that Divine Mercy is an exemplar for human mercy. When we learn from the way God deals with man, human beings can imitate God's mercy, which is his greatest attribute.[4]

We can gain this knowledge through the instrumentality of the Sacred Scriptures: The Old and The New Testaments. The early Christians and the Church

---

[3] *Laudato Si,* Apostolic Exhortation of Pope Francis. No. 13.
[4] Ibid.

Introduction

Fathers have made efforts to explain this knowledge of the mercy of God and make it intelligible for our own use.

This book is a reflection on the Divine Mercy and human activity towards the reception and dispensing of mercy. In this book, you shall learn or be reminded of the need for human mercy and the works of mercy so that we may be living witnesses of God's Mercy and our dependence on God's mercy which is boundless, as recorded in the Scriptures.

It is my desire that this book will predispose us to approach and encounter the mercy of God and strengthen our brethren in the works of mercy. I wish you many inspiring moments as you read. Happy Reading.

CHAPTER ONE

DIVINE MERCY IN THE HOLY BIBLE AND SOME FATHERS OF THE CHURCH

"No one has the capacity to judge God. We are drops in that limitless ocean of mercy."[5]

God's mercy is a monumental theme in Scripture, the English word appearing some 341 times in the Bible. The four Hebrew and three Greek words associated with this term appear a total of 454 times and are also translated as "kindness," "loving kindness," "goodness," "favor," "compassion," and "pity." Of the sixty-six books of the Bible, only sixteen do not use one of these words for mercy. Even though "mercy" is an important concept, it is somewhat difficult to prescribe a definition, especially since "grace" is occasionally closely coupled with it.

People always have this impression that the Old Testament is a part of the Bible that is filled with wrath and judgment, doom and gloom, atrocity and injustice, while the New Testament appeared to be promoting peace,

---

[5] Mahatma Gandhi, *Gandhi on Non-Violence*, New York: New Directions Publishing, 2007, p.93.

Divine Mercy in the Old Testament

"The concept of "mercy" in the Old Testament has a long and rich history."[6] In the Old Testament, *mercy*, or its English synonym, *compassion*, constitutes a fundamental attribute of the divine character, a reality highlighted in Exodus 32–34 and the account of the golden calf. Having been delivered from Egypt and given the commandments (Cf. Exodus 20:4-23), it was shocking, therefore, to discover that some forty days later Israel does the very thing that God has forbidden (Exodus 32:1–6). This single act of disobedience constitutes the breaking of the Sinai covenant, the penalty for which is death (Exodus 32:10).

The narrative continues, however. Moses intercedes for Israel and God relents from consuming the nation (Exodus 32:11–14). Moses also secures the continuation of God's guiding presence with Israel in the wilderness (Exodus 33:12–26). Then, at this point, Moses makes the startling request that God show him His glory (Exodus 33:18). Even more startling is that God agrees to do it (Exodus 33:19). The rest of the account is well-known. God hides Moses in a rock, causes His glory to pass, shows

---

[6] St. Pope John Paul II, *Dives in Misericordia*, no. 4.

Moses this divine glory, and then proclaims His name. It is this last feature that we want to consider further, the proclamation of the divine name in Exodus 34:6–7: "The Lord passed before him and proclaimed, 'The Lord, a God merciful and gracious, slow to anger, and abounding in steadfast love and faithfulness, keeping steadfast love for thousands, forgiving iniquity and transgression and sin…'"

It is truly amazing to discover, therefore, that the first thing God had determined to reveal to us about His name (or character) was that He is merciful. Of all things, He is compassionate. The Creator of heaven and earth is merciful. The One who called Abraham and delivered Israel from Egypt is compassionate.

The original context of this divine declaration helps us to understand the nature of God's mercy. Israel had sinned against God and broken His covenant with them. They deserved death, but God relented. The mercy of God in this context is exemplified by His "forgiving iniquity and transgression and sin" (Exodus 34:7). But this is not just a one-time event in order to portray one of God's "weaker" attributes. Rather, this particular attribute is central to the movement of covenantal history as portrayed in the Old Testament (Psalm 78:38; 86:15; 103:7–14), and it provides motivation for true and genuine repentance (Joel 2:12–13; 2 Chron. 30:9). See also Psalm 145:8-9 and Numbers 21:6f (How God out of His mercy saved the Israelites through the fiery serpent.)

But God's mercy is not limited to Israel in the Old Testament. Rather, it extends to all creation. Consider how Psalm 145:8 rehearses the divine attributes first recorded in Exodus 34:7 and then adds, "The Lord is good to all, and his mercy is over all that he had made" (Psalm 145:9). The biblical testimony resists a conception of God's mercy that is narrowly focused. Rather, it is a ubiquitous force that shapes all of reality, a pervasive impetus for hope.

The merciful and compassionate character of God must not remain on the dry and dusty pages of a textbook. As we have considered above, God's merciful character is translated into hope for sinners, and this is, without a doubt, the most important application of God's compassionate character. But the Bible also teaches that God's mercy and compassion reach into everyday life, especially for those who are needy and without help.

Mercy and compassion are rooted in the very character of God. His law commands it. Wisdom teaches it. The prophets enjoin it and the Psalms applaud it. It is obvious from our study that the God of the Old Testament is a merciful and compassionate God who is slow to anger and abounding in love.

Divine Mercy and Compassion in the New Testament

There is no brand-new teaching—nor a new definition of Divine Mercy to be found in the New Testament. But there is an incomparable *manifestation* of the very *depths* of God's merciful love for us through the incarnation, life, death and resurrection of His Son, Jesus Christ. This, indeed, is the underlying question that the New Testament answers for us with regard to Divine Mercy: Just how far will God go to pour out His merciful love upon mankind? As far as Bethlehem and Calvary, giving Himself without reservation to us, in human flesh—that is how far He will go!

The Gospels

Let us look first at the many gospel passages where the writers emphasize the compassion of Jesus and His tenderness for the lost and the broken, a tenderness which manifests His merciful love.

1. Christ's compassion for human physical needs in the feeding of the thousands of people (Matthew 15:32) and the healing of the two blind men (Matthew 20:34).

2. Christ's compassion for human emotional and social needs in the case of the widow of Nain and her son who was raised to life (Luke 7:13) and those hungry for the word. (Mark 6:34) Regarding the parable of the prodigal

son (Luke 15:1f), Pope John II says: "This exact picture of the prodigal son's state of mind enables us to understand exactly what the mercy of God consists in."[7]

3. Christ's compassion for those needy in every respect by healing the leper (Mark 1:40).

4. Christ's tender compassion for human grief and mortality in the case of Lazarus who was dead (John 11:32-36) and the parable of the adulterous woman (John 7:53, 8:11f).

The gospel writers tell us through passages such as mentioned above, the tender compassion of Jesus as demonstrated towards sinners and people suffering from all kinds of afflictions. The Gospel writers tell us that merciful, compassionate love was a consistent and abiding characteristic of the whole life of Jesus of Nazareth, the Son of God. And this tells us something very important about God - that he is merciful and compassionate.

St. Paul on Divine Mercy

Saint Paul gives us the most comprehensive doctrine of Divine Mercy. For him, Divine Mercy, considered as God's merciful love toward human beings, is essentially synonymous with God Himself. For example, he begins his second epistle to the Corinthians with the words: "Blessed

---

[7] St. Pope John Paul II, *Dives in Misericordia*, no. 6.

be the God and Father of our Lord Jesus Christ, the Father of mercies and the God of all comfort" (2 Corinthians 1:3).

But God, who is rich in mercy, out of the great love with which he loved us, even when we were dead through our trespasses, made us alive again with Christ (by grace you have been saved), and raised us up with Him, and made us sit with Him in the heavenly places in Christ Jesus, that in the coming ages He might show the immeasurable riches of his grace and kindness toward us in Christ Jesus (Ephesians 2: 4-7).

Perhaps the most memorable of all of St. Paul's words in this regard, are his words concerning the merciful love of Jesus Christ manifested in His death on the Cross for us:

> While we were still weak, at the right time Christ died for the ungodly. Why, one will hardly die for a righteous man — though perhaps for a good man one will dare even to die. But God shows his love for us in that while we were yet sinners, Christ died for us. Since, therefore, we are now justified by his blood, much more shall we be saved by him from the wrath of God. For if while we were enemies we were reconciled to God by the death of his Son, much more, now that we are reconciled, shall we be saved by his life. Not only that, but we also rejoice in God through our Lord Jesus Christ,

through whom we have now received our reconciliation.[8]

In fact, St. Paul's thoughts here find an echo in the book of Hebrews, which describes Jesus as "a merciful and faithful High Priest before God" (Hebrews 2:17), precisely because Jesus has made the perfect atoning sacrifice for our sins on the Cross.

Saint Paul then bases the moral imperatives that he teaches on this Gospel of Mercy — as God through Christ has been merciful to us, so we also ought to be merciful to one another: "Let all bitterness and wrath and anger and clamour and slander be put away from you, with all malice, and be kind to one another, tenderhearted, forgiving one another, as God in Christ forgave you" (Ephesians 4:31-32). Similarly, St. Paul writes in Colossians: "Put on then, as God's chosen ones, holy and beloved, compassion [the Greek phrase here is *splagchna eleous*, mercy from the very depths or guts], kindness, lowliness, meekness, and patience, forbearing one another, and, if one has a complaint against each other, forgiving each other; as the Lord has forgiven you, so you must also forgive" (Colossians 3:12).

Finally, for St. Paul, God's mercy is seen in the epistle to the Romans as the only possible explanation of why the whole human race — both Jew and Gentile alike — fall

---

[8] Romans 5:6-11.

into sin: "For God has consigned all men to disobedience, that he might have mercy on all" (Romans 11:32). In other words, God permitted evil, sin, and unfaithfulness in order to show a mercy that was even greater than sin and death. Thus, even sin and death result in God being glorified in the end, even more so than if He had not permitted human beings to fall!

Church Fathers on the Mercy of God

St. Thomas Aquinas

St. Thomas Aquinas writes that showing mercy is therefore proper to God in a special way, for it manifests His infinite perfection, and His infinite abundance and generosity. (*Summa Theologica* II-II.30.4): "If we consider a virtue in terms of its possessor, however, we can say that mercy is the greatest of the virtues only if its possessor is himself the greatest of all beings, with no one above him and everyone beneath him." This, of course, is properly true only of God Himself. Thus, mercy is, in that sense, the greatest attribute of God.

St. Pope John Paul II

The Message of Divine Mercy has always been near and dear to me. It is as if history had inscribed it in the tragic experience of the Second World

War. In those difficult years it was a particular support and an inexhaustible source of hope, not only for the people of Krakow but for the entire nation. This was also my personal experience, which I took with me to the See of Peter and which in a sense forms the image of this Pontificate.[9]

Inspired by the message of Divine Mercy, which God revealed through Sister Faustina, John Paul II wrote the Encyclical, *Dives in Misericordia*, the first in the history of the Church to be devoted to Divine Mercy; introduced the feast of Divine Mercy into the Liturgy of the Church on the first Sunday after Easter; and entrusted the whole world to Divine Mercy, so that humanity could find in It salvation and the light of hope.

Pope Francis

Pope Francis says that God's mercy is indeed an abyss beyond our understanding and he himself is trying to reach souls through God's unfathomable mercy. The Pontiff recently said, "I see the Church as a field hospital after battle. It is useless to ask a seriously injured person if he has high cholesterol and about the level of his blood sugars! You have to heal his wounds. Then we can talk about everything else." Mercy is, after all, about meeting a

---

[9] These words uttered by St. Pope John Paul II at the Shrine of Divine Mercy in Krakow-Łagiewniki are key to the understanding of his life, teaching and apostolic ministry.

person where they are at – wounds and all, just as Christ meets us where we are at.

A Summary of the Papal Bull "Misericordiae Vultus" by which Pope Francis Convoked the Extra Ordinary Jubilee Year of Mercy

On Saturday, 11th of April 2015, the Vigil of the Feast of Divine Mercy, Pope Francis promulgated the papal document that officially declared the Extraordinary Jubilee Year of Mercy. The Jubilee Year ran from Dec. 8, 2015, the Solemnity of the Immaculate Conception, which also marked the 50th anniversary of the closing of the Second Vatican Council, to Nov. 20, 2016, the Solemnity of Christ the King, which was the day the door of mercy was closed. It was a sign of the Church's communion, which was also a time of great grace to express gratitude to the Blessed Trinity. Thus, he prayed that the balm of mercy may reach everyone as a sign that God's kingdom is present in our midst.

Like the cloak of Jesus which was seamlessly woven from top to bottom, without a chapter, the Holy Father makes clear in 31 pages and 25 well-articulated numbered sections which form the personification of the Father's mercy in Jesus Christ at the fullness of time. The first five sections of the book are a glossary look at the Year of Mercy in general. There is a definition of mercy seen in the eyes of the other as the bridge between God and man among others. Mercy is seen not as an abstract word, but a face to recognize, contemplate and serve. The Pope expresses his profound joy in proclaiming the Extraordinary Jubilee Year of Mercy alongside the opening of the Door of Mercy in and outside the wall in the particular Churches all over the world. The Pope entrusted the life of the Church, all humanity, and the entire world to the Lordship of Christ, asking him to pour out his mercy upon us like the morning dew, so that everyone may work together to build a brighter future" (no.5).

Pope Francis resumes the teaching of St. John XXIII, who spoke of the "medicine of mercy", and that of Paul VI who identified the spirituality of Vatican II with that of the Samaritan. The Pontiff asserts that God's mercy is concretely an expression of His omnipotence rather than his weakness. With parables such as those of the prodigal son and the lost coin, he illustrates how mercy ascertains the paternity of God and our allegiance towards him as children. This is closely followed by the notion of mercy in the Church. For him, with an ecclesiastical reference to his predecessor, St. John Paul II *Dives in Misericordiae*, the practice of mercy as the foundation of the Church's life is beyond justice. However, while lamenting the multiple oppositions to mercy in the world today, he reminds the Church of her commission to announce the mercy of God enthusiastically alongside the new evangelization (no. 10-12).

In articles 13 and 14, the Successor of Peter stresses the "how" of being merciful. These include listening, meditating and contemplation on the Word of God as well as a life journey or pilgrimage to the Holy Door which requires dedication and sacrifice. Consequently, true Christian cheerful witnessing of Christ's missionary mandate in Luke 4:18ff should be brought to the fore via the corporal and spiritual works of mercy. These aforementioned themes are particularly close to the Pope's heart as found in section number 15 because they will "reawaken our consciences that are too often grown dull in the face of poverty." The Church, the Holy Father asserts, should take the lead to healing people's wounds with the oil of consolation, bind them with mercy and cure them with solidarity vigilantly.

The Holy Father admonishes that the Lenten season during the Year of Mercy should be remarkable. The Pontiff emphasizes the need for the administration and reception of the Sacrament of Reconciliation for interior peace. Confessors are encouraged to warmly embrace the repentant son and go out to meet the elder son as an authentic sign of the Father's mercy (Luke 18:15). Consequently, the Holy Father rejoices in sending "missionaries of mercy" (no.18) to particular Churches with the faculty to pardon even sins reserved for the Holy See. While condemning corruption which he defines as "a festering wound; a grave sin that cries out to the heavens for vengeance, since it threatens the very foundation of personal and social life; an evil, a public scandal that prevents us from future hope," the Pope invites all to mercy. Let none, not even the corrupt, be restrained from or indifferent to the experience of mercy or be fooled by illusionary wealth since God's judgment is inevitable in articles 18 and 19.

Rather than a contradiction, justice and mercy are conceived as two dimensions of a reality which culminates in the fullness of love. With relevant scriptural passages, the Pontiff holds that God expresses His justice in His mercy. The cross becomes the justice and judgement of God on us all by grace since through it His love and life are offered us (nos. 20-21).

The Pope advises us to live and gain indulgences in article 22. "The freedom from the residue left by the consequences of sins for a growth in charity rather than a relapse in sin" is the Pontiff's definition of indulgence. Without limits, the Holy Father encourages a respectful dialogue with Judaism and Islam as with other religions by extension in article 23 and admonishes Christians to approach the Father's mercy with certainty that His mercy is boundless.

> I trust that this Jubilee year celebrating the mercy of God will foster an encounter with these religions and with other noble religious traditions: may it open us to even more fervent dialogue so that we might know and understand one another better, may it eliminate every form of close-

mindedness and disrespect, and drive out every form of violence and discrimination.[10]

There was recourse to the Blessed Virgin Mary, Mother of Mercy and St. Faustina Kowalska. He concludes with a reaffirmation of the superabundant reality of the mercy of God while he charges the Church to love this credibly by being an active confident voice for all mankind.

In simple terms, the Pontiff reveals the face of the Father's mercy of which he is totally convinced. The Pope wishes that this Holy Year be dedicated to living out in our daily lives the mercy which the Father constantly extends to all of us. In his words:

> Let us allow God to surprise us because he is never tired of throwing open the doors of his heart because he loves us and wants to share his love with us... In this Jubilee Year, may the church echo the word of God that resounds strong and clear signs of pardon and love. May the Church never be tired of extending mercy and be ever patient in offering compassion and comfort. May the Church become the voice of every man and woman and repeat confidently without end: Be

---

[10] no. 23

mindful of your mercy, O Lord and your steadfast love, for they have been from of old. [11]

Consequent upon the relevance of the message eminent in this Bull of the Pontiff, I recommend it to all cleric and lay faithful, as well as to all men and women of good will, for their spiritual benefits, not only during the year of mercy but at all times for a better human society that appreciates the role of mercy in human relationships and also in our relationship with God.

The convocation of the Extra Ordinary Jubilee Year of Mercy by Pope Francis is not only a clarion call for the reawakening of the consciousness of God's boundless mercy and love for His people, but a pathway towards the re-visitation of the mercy of God which resonates through the Scriptures. The word of God is a seed containing God's fullness and His abounding love for humanity that bears much fruit when understood and obeyed. The Old and the New Testaments' documents are in no small measure, the reality of God's Mercy. They culminate in the affirmative views of the Fathers of the Church on Divine Mercy.

---

[11]https://www.thedivinemercy.org/library/article.php?NID=6281, accessed on 29/8/2018.

Conclusion

It is obvious from our study that the Old and New Testaments are united in their affirmation that the God of the Bible is a merciful and compassionate God. In fact, it would be appropriate to characterize the entire Bible as a book that journals God's mercy and compassion. The aforementioned Fathers of the Church were unanimous in their affirmation that our God is a God of mercy and compassion. This God of mercy and compassion also calls us, His people, to exemplify these attributes in our own lives. He has been merciful to us. We bear forth the image of this mercy to the world. We are called to "give justice to the weak and the fatherless; to maintain the right of the afflicted and the destitute, to rescue the weak and the needy and to deliver them from the hand of the wicked" (Psalm 82:3–4).

Indeed, the undeniable mercy of God has been revealed in his word and this also finds expression in the words of the Fathers of the Church. Christians are therefore called to engage too in the diverse works of mercy that would reflect the physical manifestation of the mercy of God. In this way, humanity will experience genuine love in their daily relationship with Christians all over the world. This would be fully realized if Christians faithfully execute the spiritual and corporal works of mercy as presented by the Church. The next chapter seeks to unravel the role of the spiritual works of mercy in establishing God's kingdom here on earth and forgiving others as we have undeservedly obtained mercy.

CHAPTER TWO
SPIRITUAL WORKS OF MERCY

Introduction

In our review of the Bull of Indiction, *Misericordiae Vultus,* of the Extraordinary Jubilee Year of Mercy by Pope Francis, we mentioned that the spiritual works and the corporal works of mercy are very central to the Pope's reflection. In our last chapter on the Divine Mercy in the Bible, we reiterated the importance of witnessing to the mercy of God in our own time, especially during the Year of Mercy. For the purpose of this chapter, we shall examine the spiritual works of mercy as a way of being merciful like God our Father.

The spiritual works of mercy have long been a part of the Christian tradition, appearing in the works of theologians and spiritual writers throughout history. Just as Jesus attended to the spiritual well-being of those He ministered to, these spiritual works of mercy guide us to "help our neighbours in their spiritual needs." The seven spiritual works of mercy are listed below. After each work of mercy there are also suggestions and words of advice for living them out in our daily lives.[12]

1. Counselling the Doubtful

(1 Corinthians 1:25; Proverbs 19:20)

Everyone has moments of doubt in their faith journey. Nevertheless, we should always remember that Christ is the Way, the Truth, and the Life, and that no one can come to the Father except through Him. Hence, we must turn to Him in prayer and always turn to Him in our journey through life. There are so many ways we can counsel the doubtful. The following may be useful tips on how we can effectively do this as Christians:

- "Listen to counsel and receive instruction, that you may eventually become wise" (Proverbs 19:20).
- The Cross of Christ "the foolishness of God is wiser than human wisdom, and the weakness of God is stronger than human strength" (1 Corinthians 1:25).

---

[12]See http://www.usccb.org/beliefs-and-teachings/how-we-teach/new-evangelization/jubilee-of-mercy/the-spiritual-works-of-mercy.cfm, accessed on 29/08/2018.

- Has someone asked you for advice? Orient your response to Christ, who is the Way, the Truth, and the Life.
- Follow Christ with the witness of your life so that others may see God's love revealed in your actions.
- Accompany a friend who is struggling with believing to join a parish group for service or faith formation, share a book you found useful in dealing with your friend's faith concern, and worship at Sunday Mass.

2. Admonishing the Sinner

(Matthew 18:15-20; Colossians 3:5-17; 1 Thessalonians 5:12, 2 Thessalonians 3:15)

The above scriptural passages make lucid the Christian foundation of this duty.

> If your brother should commit some wrong against you, go and point out his fault, but keep it between the two of you. If he listens to you, you have won your brother over. If he does not listen, summon another, so that every case may stand on the word of two or three witnesses. If he ignores them, refer it to the Church (Matthew 18:15-17a).

This passage is worthy of citation because it vehemently expresses one's duty to reconcile with another person who offends him. It is in a sense an act of admonition. St. Paul's letter to the Colossians 3:15 explains quite succinctly the importance of the work of a Christian to admonish the sinner: "Christ's peace must reign in your hearts, since as members of the one body you have been called to that peace."

Admonishing the sinner as a spiritual work of mercy is a very vital element in Christian living in our contemporary world, where the attitude of individualism seems to have crept into our cultures. The importance and relevance of admonishing the sinner is not only hinged on the fact that this should be a mere Christian obligation, "they (the other spiritual works of mercy inclusive) also have broader social and political implications today and are to be linked in many cases with the overriding demands of social justice."[13]

As was mentioned earlier, individualism is gradually becoming the order of the day; people do not care for the concerns of their neighbours, let alone strangers. This spiritual work of mercy is a call to Christians; it is a reminder that the Church makes to Christ's faithful not to forget the instructions of Christ himself. It is important to admonish the sinner because many of the actions of some people are carried out in ignorance, or in confusion. They

---

[13] Richard McBrien, *Catholicism*, New York: Harper San Francisco, 1994, P. 942.

need someone to counsel them even without their knowing. When this supposed counselor is not forth coming, the grief of their wrong doing could culminate in them committing suicide or constantly drifting into sin. Others might just be aware of their actions, but the constant counsel of a Christian as in Matthew 18:15-17, may just stop them from continuing.

We all ought to live in harmony. Some people, Christians at that, nurse the wrong done to them and keep malice for days, weeks, months, even years, without letting their offenders know their annoyance. This is what this spiritual work of mercy demands of us, to confront our offenders and not to wait for them to come to tender an apology. St. Paul adds "but do not treat him like an enemy; rather, correct him as you would a brother" (2 Thessalonians 3:15). This work of mercy calls both parties to cultivate the virtue of humility. Humility is essential to faith. Pride is the reason why people refuse to do what they are expected to do as Christians. No one without humility would or can freely carryout the demands of this spiritual work of mercy. Humility involves glorying in the Cross of Christ. "To glory in the wisdom of Christ is no great thing, but to glory in the Cross of Christ is a great thing."[14]

This spiritual work of mercy is a call to all Christians to actively partake in Christ's act of loving. For to be humble, as to call your offender and admonish him/her,

---

[14] St. Augustine, *The Christian Life*, compiled by Anthony Tonna-Barthet, J.F McGowan (trans.), New York: Frederich Pustet Co. (Inc) 1929. P.127.

demands true followership of Christ. Let us shun the attitude of individualism and be open to one another. Let us live as the early Christians lived in harmony and unity. This spiritual work of mercy equally affects our political world today. Our religious leaders are challenged to call on our political leaders to stop their corrupt, immoral practices which harm the life of all in the society. In the light of performing their spiritual obligation, let them admonish those leaders who offend the populace by their actions. We are also called upon to carry out this work of mercy at home, in school, in work places, on the streets and wherever and whenever possible.

3. Instructing the Ignorant

(Romans 11:25; 1Corinthians 10:1; 1Timothy 4:6-16; 2Timothy 4:1-5; 1Thessalonians 4:13)

St. Paul asks: "But how are men to believe of whom they have never heard? And how are they to hear without a preacher..." (Romans 10: 14-15). "My people perish for lack of knowledge" (Hosea 4:6). Knowledge here means a lot. It denotes spiritual knowledge of God and other forms of knowledge. People are used to saying that 'ignorance is the worst of all diseases,' thus if you want to liberate a man, you educate the man. This is exactly the aim of this spiritual work of mercy. This is no doubt the intention of St. Paul in his second letter to Timothy. "In the presence of God and of Christ Jesus, who is coming to judge the living and the dead and by his appearing and his kingly power, I charge you to heal the world, to stay with this task whether convenient or inconvenient - correcting, reporting, appealing-constantly teaching and never losing patience" (2 Timothy 4:1-2).

To be ignorant is to be bereft of knowledge of something and thus makes one in need or want of knowledge or else they will suffer for the gap created by their ignorance of a thing. "There is no knowledge of God in the land... Therefore, the land mourns, and everything that dwells in it languished" (Hosea 4:1-3). This scriptural passage could be said to mean that the primary knowledge that man should possess is the knowledge of God, after which comes all other forms of knowledge. The knowledge of God is a foundation upon which all other kinds of knowledge are built. If this vital knowledge is lacking, then the case of Hosea 4:3 will be the result. This is a call on the need for missionary activities to be intensified. It is quite embarrassing, when someone is regarded as an illiterate, unable to read or write; but it is more devastating when one is ignorant of God. This spiritual work of mercy is so designed to eliminate this menace (ignorance of God). To carry out this work of mercy, is to embark on evangelization. This is not restricted to preaching the gospel, but it begins from it. Christians, in fulfilling their religious duty, should "go all out" to preach Christ to the world. The aim of giving instruction is to create information and to correct misunderstandings and prejudices that occur on account of ignorance. Instruction helps people to see things from a different point of view and invites them to conversion. To instruct the ignorant is to simply make them understand what they misunderstood, showing realities to them from a different point of view. This can go a long way to make all the world to grow in knowledge and wisdom.

4. Comforting the Sorrowful

(Romans 12:15; Revelations 21:4; Psalm 34:18)

In the life of each one of us, there are good and bad moments; what we refer to as the vicissitude of life for humankind. In such moments we are called to be open to listening and comforting those who are dealing with grief. Even if we aren't sure of the right words to say, our presence can make a big difference and help in bringing consolation to those in grief.

- Lend a listening ear to those going through a tough time.
- Make a home cooked meal for a friend who is facing a difficult time.
- Write a letter or send a card to someone who is suffering.

- A few moments of your day may make a lifetime of difference to someone who is going through a difficult time.

5. Bearing Wrongs Patiently

(Matthew 16:24; James 5:7-11)

"It requires fortitude to endure strain, stress, and evil without causing more suffering and evil. Humility is to help a person keep the underlying needs of others in mind when their needs are inadequately or inappropriately expressed and when there are no immediate or easy solutions."[15]

This spiritual work of mercy demands that one bears wrong accusations, insults and all false allegations channeled against him. The virtue of patience is called to action here. This virtue of bearing wrongs patiently is precisely what Jesus asks of His disciples when He said, "if any want to become my followers, let them deny themselves and take up their cross and follow me" (Matthew 16:24).

It is quite painful and very disheartening when a false accusation is brought against you. It is one of the most painful and terrible ways to hurt someone. And yet it is demanded of Christians to bear such accusations patiently.

---

[15] Ibid.

Indeed, the practice of Christianity is difficult, but its teachings are worth trying. Following from this, Jesus says that who wishes to become His disciple must carry his cross.

It is indeed not an easy task, to bear wrong patiently, knowing especially that you are innocent. Is this not a means of dying in silence when you should rather speak up? Is it not silent stupidity? Definitely, it is in the eyes of the world, but not so in the eyes of God. Bearing wrongs patiently demands that one does not just get angry about wrongs done you. "Place your hope in God so that you can endure the troubles of this world and face them with a compassionate spirit."[16] This is an easy way to face such annoying circumstances.

The letter of James 5:7-11 gives us more concrete reasons why it is not stupid and dying in stupidity to bear wrongs patiently:

> Be patient; therefore, beloved, until the coming of the Lord. The farmer waits for the precious crop from the earth, being patient with it receives the early and the late rains. You also must be patient... do not grumble against one another... As an example of suffering and patience, beloved, take the prophets who spoke in the name of the Lord.

---

[16]http://www.usccb.org/beliefs-and-teachings/how-we-teach/new-evangelization/jubilee-of-mercy/the-spiritual-works-of-mercy.cfm, Accessed on 16/5/16.

Indeed, we call blessed those who showed endurance. You have heard of the endurance of Job, and you have seen the purpose of the Lord, how the Lord is compassionate and merciful.

This clearly tells us of the need to be patient with one another just as God is patient with us. If we are sinners in need of God's mercy, why can't we show mercy by being patient with our neighbors or those who offend us? Be not like the wicked servant who was shown mercy yet refused to show mercy afterwards (Mathew 18:25-34). Patience is thus a necessary virtue we need as Christians. We need patience because situations will surely come in our lives, when we must bear wrongs, and this we must do patiently.

6. Forgiving Injuries

(Matthew 6:15; 18:21-35; Colossians 3:13)

Ordinarily, our Christian sensitivity is directed towards love, love of God and neighbour; and where there is love there is bound to be harmony because love keeps no score of wrongs. Thus, it follows that Christians ordinarily should be merciful, just as their heavenly Father is merciful (Luke 6:36), forgiving one another and living in unity. This is the demand of this spiritual work of mercy. "Forgiving others is difficult at times because we do not have God's limitless mercy and compassion. But Jesus teaches us that we should forgive as God forgives, relying on him to help us show others the mercy of God... forgiveness transforms hearts and lives."[17] Forgiveness is one means through which we partake or participate in the Sacrament of Penance. It is an act that once again fulfills what God intends for us: to be like Him, who is all forgiving. We should avail ourselves of this opportunity.

In Matthew 6:15, Scripture states: "But if you do not forgive others, neither will your Father forgive your trespasses." This is an indication to how important forgiveness is. God wants us to forgive others as much as we can because forgiveness is healing. There may be obvious circumstances that are very hurtful and may seem closed to forgiveness. But if God, who is our heavenly Father, forgives us for any wrong and invites us to be merciful as He is, why shouldn't we. We may feel hurt, but we should not let sunset find us still angry (Ephesians 4:26). Learn to forgive and let go. One can be angry, that is a human quality, but do not keep grudges. Jesus tells his disciples to forgive one another as many as seventy-seven times (Matthew 18:21).

It is very necessary to build a culture of forgiveness about ourselves; this is important because it lessens our burdens and enables us to work more dedicatedly. Holding an injury against someone is not different from holding a curse against that person. Such a person will be troubled

---

[17] Ibid.

and distressed. He will be filled with guilt and might even be led to suicidal actions. Thus, forgiveness is a prerequisite for happiness, unity, harmony and peace among a people.

The Church was not mistaken when she included the act of forgiveness as one of the spiritual works of mercy that her faithful must practice. It is an action which concretely draws us or connects us with God our Father and defines our likeness with Him more distinctly.

7. Praying for the Living and the Dead

(James 5:16; Colossians 3; 9; II Maccabeus 12:45)

Prayer is the means through which we communicate our troubles and concerns to God. God Himself has given us the opportunity to interact with him by sending his Son, Jesus Christ, to teach us how to pray. Therefore, it is our duty as Christians to pray without ceasing.

As much as we pray for our (living) needs, we must also endeavour to pray for the dead. This practically means that the act of praying for the living and the dead is a typical expression of the unity of the Church. The Church teaches that there are three basic entities which comprise her membership: The Church triumphant (the Saints), the Church militant (the living) and the Church suffering (the dead). Christians are thus to pray to the Saints to intercede on behalf of the living and the dead. Only the Church militant can visibly pray.

In other words, Christians on earth are the tools or the means through which prayers can be asked for from God through the Saints for the living and for the dead, who are in dire need of our prayers. By the dead here, reference is being made to the souls in purgatory. Hence, Christians must not get tired of praying. Considering the value of prayer, it suffices to say that Christians should pray when they sit in their house, and when they walk, when they lie down and when they rise.

One might ask, "Why should we pray for the dead?" Are they not dead and thus have no connection with us (living) anymore? The dead dearly need our prayers. "He made atonement for the dead, so that they might be delivered from their sin" (II Maccabeus 12:45). It is our prayers more than their suffering that will cleanse them of their sins and take them to be with God in heavenly ecstasy. In equal parlance, we are not to limit our prayers for our fellow brethren. We must pray earnestly and constantly for the good of one another and for the world, that God's true mission may be accomplished on earth. St. Paul wrote to the Colossians in this regard, "for this reason, since the day we heard it, we have not ceased praying for you and asking that you may be filled with the knowledge of God's will in all spiritual wisdom and understanding" (Colossians 1:9). Our prayers should be edifying and not to limit one another. "In our prayers for you we always thank God, the

Father of our Lord Jesus Christ" (Colossians 1:3). The Church has rightly requested us to prove our Christian worth by this simple function of prayer - praying for your neighbor. It is an indication of charity to which Jesus calls us to be active participants.

Conclusion

From the foregoing, it is glaring that the spiritual needs of those around us are very important, in a bid to establish God's kingdom here on earth by being living witnesses and examples of His Divine Mercy. Through the spiritual works of mercy, we draw humanity closer to the God of all grace and love. This however, is one part of a complete whole of our Christian calling, for man has both spiritual and physical needs. Man consists of both physical (body) and spiritual (soul). Therefore, the spiritual works of mercy should lead seamlessly to a conscious effort to also perform the corporal works as both are the revelation of God's love for humanity, made visible in our works on earth towards the poor and the needy and humanity in general. The next chapter would examine the seven corporal works of mercy.

CHAPTER THREE
CORPORAL WORKS OF MERCY

Introduction

"You will achieve more in this world through acts of mercy than you will through acts of retribution."[18] The works of mercy have simply become indispensable and irreplaceable, considering the increase in the population of the internally displaced persons, the high number of the refugee camps we have today and indeed the hardship resulting from the insufficiency of many, both immediate and remote. The onus therefore lies on all of us to yield to the clarion call to 'go all out' and carry out the works of mercy. This is with reference to concrete works that we carry out as Christians, that which, St. James demands when he writes: "faith without work is dead" (James 2: 26), "show me your faith and I will show you my work" (James 2:18). On another occasion, St. James says: "God bless you" is not enough to assuage a hungry man. We must work.

---

[18]http://www.unfoundation.org/blog/12-nelson-mandela-quotes.html, accessed on 28/08/2018.

The above desire and vision of St. James, point to nothing other than the consideration of the corporal works of mercy. Corporal works of mercy "are charitable actions by which we help our neighbors in their bodily needs."[19] The corporal works of mercy are also physical and sometimes referred to as human mercy, which finds fulfillment only in relation to God's mercy. Karl Rahner has this to say:

> All human mercy is founded and summoned forth by that of God. It can only be called mercy (in an analogical sense) as a response, because it knows that its own self and all it has to give are always received by way of a loan; so that human mercy does not give of its own but only what it has received, and that not at will but because God's mercies to a man always compel him in turn to show mercy. Mercy sees the distress of others as its own.[20]

Rahner is simply portraying the fact that human mercy comes from God and must be carried out by all.

But to whom shall we perform the works of mercy? "One should help those who cannot sufficiently help themselves, not those whose need results from ongoing

---

[19] See *United States Catechism for Adults*, Washington, DC: United States Conference of Catholic Bishops, 2006.
[20] Karl Rahner (ed.) *Encyclopedia of Theology*. Germany: Burns and Oates, 1975, p. 954, S.V. 'Mercy'.

unwillingness to do what they can and should be doing."[21] St. Paul was unequivocal in this regard. He writes: "Anyone unwilling to work should not eat" (2 Thessalonians 3:10). Those who cannot help themselves here are the poor - this "class of people of any age, color, position, race and in any country, designated as living below a certain set of visible and spiritual standards."[22] For "our faith in Christ, who became poor, and was always close to the poor and the outcast, is the basis of our concern for the integral development of society's most neglected members."[23] Indeed, true faith in the incarnate Son of God is inseparable from self-giving.[24]

The poor can also be seen as the less privileged. This group is the set that we must direct our corporal works of mercy to, for Pope Francis encourages: "We have to state without mincing words that there is an inseparable bond between our faith and the poor. May we never abandon them."[25]

The Catholic Church, relying on the scriptural provision has identified the works we carry out to fulfill the

---

[21] Germain Grizez, *The May of the Lord Jesus: Difficult Moral questions*, Illinois: Franciscan Press, 1997, p. 436.
[22] Rodney J. Hunter, *Dictionary of Pastoral Care and Counselling*, Nashville: Abingdon Press, 1990, p. 926.
[23] Pope Francis, *Evangelii Gaudium*, no. 186.
[24] *Ibid.*, no. 88.
[25] *Ibid., no 88-89.*

corporal demands of the needy. "The list is long established," J. M. Perrim writes.[26] The list includes:

1. Feed the Hungry
2. Give Water to the Thirsty
3. Bury the Dead
4. Visit the Sick
5. Clothe the Naked
6. Harbor the Homeless
7. Comfort the Prisoner

1. Feed the Hungry

(Matthew 25:35; Isaiah 58:10)

We must reflect on the questions: What is hunger? Why must it be satisfied?

Certainly, "food is among the most essential and most basic needs and hunger is the most difficult and pressing cry of the body for food."[27]

Food gives life to man by strengthening and sustaining man with its nutrients. Dolores observes:

---

[26] J. M. Perrin, "Works of Mercy" in *New Catholic Encyclopedia*, vol. ix. Washington DC: Jack Heraty and Associates Inc., 1967.
[27] George Kaitholil, *Mercy; Divine and Human,* Mumbai: St. Pauls Publications, 2015, p. 49.

Nature intended us to nourish ourselves with actual food... Food after all, contains both the nutrients that have been discovered and those that have not; some of a food's benefits may as yet be unknown, and the synergism of its combined elements is not contained on the necessity of food for nutrient saying: Every food we put into our bodies contains nutrients and chemicals that act on it in ways that will be important to us, if not today or tomorrow, then some years soon.[28]

By the fact of human nature, every man depends on food. To deny anybody of food therefore, is to kill such a person. However, it is not everything that is edible. William Barclay makes a very important observation that we must also take note: "all food and vegetables were clean before presenting it."[29]

Our Lord Jesus Christ clearly understood this necessity of food in human existence over 2000 years ago. This is why He did not allow his disciples to be condemned when they broke the Sabbath law in the field of wheat (Luke 6:1f). In fact, Jesus even alluded to David's entrance into the Tabernacle to eat the food that is meant for the priests, in response to the Pharisees, thus, relaxing the law about Sabbath because of food. Jesus fed the multitude and gave

---

[28] Dolores Riccio, *Supper Food for Women,* New York: Warner Books, 1996, p. 8.
[29] William Barclay, *The New Daily Study Bible, the Gospel of Matthew, Bangalore:* Theological Publications in India, 2009, p. 130.

the food of life, the bread that comes from heaven (John 6:1-15).

Food is so important for our Lord Jesus Christ, that, this was the form in which he chose to perpetuate His presence for humanity. He achieved this through the institution of the Sacrament of the Holy Eucharist. "In this Sacrament," Pope Benedict XVI wrote: "The Lord truly becomes food for us, to satisfy our hunger for... freedom... Christ becomes for us the food of truth."[30]

We all ask for this bread and Jesus, in fact, encourages us to do so, when he gave the pattern of all prayers.

> "Our daily bread" (in the Lord's Prayer) refers to the earthly nourishment necessary to everyone for subsistence and also to the bread of life... while we seek what we need for our maintenance and development, we must never forget the poor of the world, who often lack daily bread.[31]

Like the Jews in the time of Jesus, many people today continue to say: "Please, give us this bread every day" (John 6:34). Jesus, on His part, continues to beckon to us as he did to His apostles saying, "You yourself give them something to eat" (Matthew 6:37). We must continually join Christ, who is the Bread of Life, to give food to the hungry even as he says to everyone in the person of Peter,

---

[30] Benedict XVI, *Sacramentum Caritatis,* no. 2.
[31] *United States Catholic Catechism for Adults*, p. 487.

to "feed my sheep" (John 21:16). We are encouraged to care for one another, especially those who are in need. This is the only way we can answer the question posed to Cain and as the Lord continues to say to us: "Where is your brother?" (Genesis 4). Food sustains life and gives strength. In our missionary journey to the world, let us continue to give food to the hungry.

We should desire and say with the Brazilian Bishops:

> We wish to take up daily the joys and hopes, the difficulties and sorrows of the ... people...lacking food and health care – to the detriment of their rights. Seeing their poverty, hearing their cries and knowing their sufferings, we are scandalized because we know that there is enough food for everyone and that this is the result of poor distribution of foods and income.[32]

We should also heed the voice of Pope John XXIII, who pushed this further when he wrote: "Yet we desire more than this; ... we are not simply talking about ensuring nourishment or a dignified sustenance for all people but also for their general temporal welfare and prosperity."[33] If we heed the voice of this Holy Father, in addition to giving food, we will also balance people's physical and psychological disorder, since, "most cases of food

---

[32] Conferencia Nacional Dos Bispos Do Brazil, Ezigencias Evangelicans e Eticas De Superecao Miseria E da Fome, 2002, no. 2.
[33] John XXIII, *Encyclical Letter, Mater et Magistra*, 1961, no 3

intolerance are not due to allergy. The most common cause of an aversion to food is psychological."[34] Beloved, you may not be able to feed everybody, but if you can feed some, what stops you?

2. Give drink to the thirsty

(Matthew 25:31-40; Matthew 10:42)

"Whoever gives a cup of water to this little one on the account of me will not lose the reward" (Matthew 10: 42).

In addition to the food we give, we must also give water, which is life for them to drink. It is the utmost desire of our Lord Jesus Christ that we should have water to drink. He Himself gives us an example to follow. This is magnificently demonstrated in the water that flows from the side of Jesus when He was paying the price of our redemption on the cross of Calvary (John 19).

Despite this radical demonstration, the Bible is replete with Jesus' instruction, calling us to give water to our neighbour. In the first place, Jesus includes in the criteria for us to enjoy the eternal life with Him, the giving of water to the thirsty. He says: "When I was thirsty, you gave me water to drink. Now come into the house of my father" (Matthew 25:35). Again, in another passage of the Bible,

---

[34] Jacob C. Handelsman (ed.), *The Concise Medical Encyclopedia*, S. V. 'Food', New York: Ottenheimer Pub Co, 1998.

He says that anyone who gives a cup of water to this little one on the account of me shall not lose his reward (Matthew 10:42).

The idea of water in our Christian faith and spirituality is superb and interesting. Consider for instance, the water of Baptism. I have heard people say: "What binds us together is stronger than what separates us." Baptism in our faith is the Sacrament that makes us children of God and members of Christ's body. It is the water of this Sacrament of Baptism that binds us together. This water is said to be thicker and even stronger than blood. Anytime we give water to the thirsty, we strengthen our union with Christ, His Church and our fellow human beings. We must never cease to give this water.

Every time we give water to the thirsty in the name of Christ, our master, it matters not to whom we give it; the water we give is that which flows from the holy temple. This water, which flows from the temple to other rivers, becomes the water of healing, recreation and regeneration. By so doing, we become the temple of the Lord and our hearts, the altar. Those we give the water to will become other channels to dispense the goodness of this river.

Jesus Himself is the water of life. He revealed this during the discussion with the Samaritan woman who begged: "Sir, give me this water, that I may not thirst, nor come here to draw" (John 4:15). She made this appeal because Jesus had said: "Everyone who drinks the water will be thirsty again but whoever drinks the water I shall give will never thirst; the water I shall give will become in him the spring of water welling up to eternal life" (John 4: 13-14).

To us human beings, water is very important. Our dear Holy Father, Pope Francis, underscores this succinctly: "Fresh drinking water is an issue of primary importance, since it is indispensable for human life and for supporting terrestrial and adequate ecosystem. Sources of fresh water are necessary for health care, agriculture and industry."[35] However important is water for human existence, the availability and supply of water is not encouraging in some places in recent times. Pope Francis again creates an insight:

> Water supply used to be relatively constant, but now in many places demand exceeds the sustainable supply, with dramatic consequences in the short and long term. Large citrus dependent on significant supplies of water have experienced periods of shortage...[36]

As for the shortage of water, the Holy Father makes a pointer to yet another aspect concerning the issue of water. He writes: "One particular serious problem is the quality of water available to the poor."[37] He continues by saying: "Underground water sources in many places are threatened

---

[35] Pope Francis, Encyclical Letter, *Laudato Si,* no. 28.
[36] Ibid.
[37] Ibid no. 29.

by the pollution produced in certain mining, farming, and industrial activities, especially in countries lacking adequate regulation or control."[38]

If we continue with the above situation described by Pope Francis, the consequence is not farfetched. The Holy Father says: "Greater scarcity of water will lead to an increase in the cost of food and various products which depend on its use. Some studies warn that an acute water shortage may occur within a few decades unless urgent action is taken."[39] This is evidently correct and lucid even to the unlettered because, "everyday, unsafe water results in many deaths and the spread of water related diseases...Dysentery and cholera, linked to inadequate hygiene and water supplies, are a significant cause of suffering and infant mortality."[40]

It is in this light and within this context that we all must respond to this call from Macedonia and give good water to the thirsty. Indeed we must bear in mind that "our world owes a grave social debt towards the poor, who lack access to drinking water, because they are denied the right to a life consistent with their inalienable dignity."[41] To pay this debt adequately we must realize that "access to safe drinkable water is a basic and universal human right, since it is essential to human survival and, as such, is a condition for

---

[38] Ibid.
[39] Ibid no. 31.
[40] Ibid no. 29.
[41] Ibid no. 30.

the exercise of other human rights."[42] Beloved, when we give water to the thirsty, we give life; we give Jesus, who shall give us the living water. Let us not grow tired therefore, of doing this good. May Christ, the source of the eternal living water, continue to satisfy our thirst.

3. Bury the Dead

(Genesis 3:19; 23:4; Deuteronomy 21:23)

"In many ways, we are most human when we bury our loved ones."[43] The inevitability of death has been proven beyond reasonable doubt. Anyone who is totally skeptical about this fact can be likened to a fool or a less knowledgeable fellow. This is because such a person is not aware of the finitude of man. We cannot deny the fact that "all men are mortal."[44] The philosopher Martin Heidegger puts it more forcefully by pointing out that man is 'being - towards death' as presented by W. Lawhead. In fact, human freedom for Heidegger is "freedom towards death."[45] It is part of human nature to die.

---

[42] Ibid.
[43] Mark O. Ikeke, *Race and Racism (a Socio-Political and Philosophic Anthropology,* Awka, Nigeria: Fab Educational Books, 2011, p. 41.
[44] William Lawhead, The Voyage of Discovery, Ohio: Wadsworth, 2002, p. 541.
[45] *Being and Time* transl. by John Macquarries and Edward Robinson, London: S.C.M. Press, 1962, p.311.

However, "...death is one phenomenon that summarizes an entrance into the extra – territoriality: it is the relocation into the non-location."[46] By this, one passes from visibility to invisibility, mortality to immortality, limitedness to 'unlimitedness.' "... For the doctor, death occurs when a patient stops breathing completely. Put differently, when the bio-chemical organs of the human body collapse and become totally irretrievable and irreparable."[47] In this sense, the human being has stopped existing in the normal and ordinary human existence; he/she has changed the mode of life. The book of Wisdom puts it very well, "...life is not ended, it is only changed" (Wisdom 3:15).

Although, this change has become part of human nature, it was not there before. St. Ambrose of Milan represents the Christian view vividly when he wrote: "God did not ordain death in the beginning of things, but he gave it to us as a remedy when that damnable sin brought toil and tears into human life. This sorrow had to be brought to an end so that death can bring back what life has thrown away."[48] Notwithstanding the initial part of the quotation above by St. Ambrose, the other part points to the fact that

---

[46] Emmanuel Franklyne Ogbunwuezeh, "Death in Igbo Conceptual Schemes - a Therapy of myth, Mystery and Metaphysics" in *The Kpim of Death Essays in Memory of Rev. Fr. Prof. Panteleon Iroegbu*, edited by George Uzoma, Bloomington: Trafford Publishing, 2007, p. 20.
[47] Francis Ogunmodede in, George Uzoma Ukagba (ed), *Kpim of Death*, Bloomington: Trafford Publishing, 2007, p. 29.
[48] See the Book of St. Ambrose of Milan on the Death of his Brother Sarryrus, Book 2, Read in Divine Office Vol. 3 974, pp.378-379.

death is a gift from God and has become part of human nature.

Closely knit with this inevitable event in human existence is burial of the dead. It is, however, not part of the criteria for eternal bliss, given by Jesus Christ in Matthew chapter 25. However, the Catholic tradition has counted the act of burying the dead as part of the corporal works of mercy. Mark O. Ikeke says: "In many ways we are most human when we bury our loved ones."[49] The question: 'Is it only our loved ones that we are to bury?' may arise. I will say No. This is because we are supposed to love everybody. That is to say that this must be done without favouritism. Whenever we favour one over the other, in the case of a burial, we deny the other person a proper burial. I believe that "the human person is also depersonalized when he is denied a befitting burial."[50]

As a matter of fact, to bury the dead is part of the natural responsibility of man. While considering the works of Cornel West, Mark O. Ikeke writes: "Arguing from the etymological root... the word human is from the Latin word *humanitas,* which means 'to bury."[51] When we consider this linguistic aspect of human reality, I doubt if there can be any rational justification to explain away the responsibility of burying the dead. What is left is the

---

[49] Mark O. Ikeke, *Race and Racism (A Socio-Political and Philosophic Anthropology),* p.41.
[50] Ibid.
[51] Ibid.

acceptance of this responsibility. Thus, Jesus says to all, let the dead bury the dead. 'Commonsensically', a dead person cannot perform the work of the living, that is, to bury. That will lead to contradiction. But Jesus' thought is not contradictory. The dead, who are to bury the dead here, are the living ones, for man is a being- towards-death.[52]

We must follow the example of our Lord Jesus Christ, the resurrection and Life, who has concern for the dead. This was displayed when "Jesus wept" (John 11:35) with the family of Lazarus and the encounter with the widow of Nain (Luke 7:11-17). When we bury the dead, we prepare and present their body for their resurrection by Jesus on the last day. This is exactly what Mary and Martha did to Lazarus. We must heed the clarion call to help our brothers and sisters at the time of death because "through death, our life is transformed to greater heights from mortality to immortality, from visibility to invisibility and from temporality to eternity."[53] While some are buried in a befitting manner, others are left to decompose on the surface of the earth; but we must commit all our dead to the mercy of God. So, may the souls of all the faithful departed through the mercy of God rest in peace. Amen.

---

[52] Martin Heidegger, *Being and Time*, p. 311.
[53] See Pantaleon Iroegbu Osondu, *Kpim of Time: Eternity*, Ibadan: Hope Publications, 2004.

4. Visit the Sick

(Matthew 25:36; James 5:14)

Not everyone can visit the imprisoned or those in jail, but we can visit those who are imprisoned in their minds or their bodies. No matter how they are imprisoned or locked up in themselves, whether by alcohol or drugs, by depression or darkness, by sin or the error of atheism and heresy, we can be patient and merciful and present to them.[54]

The sick people in our society are those who are infected with one disease or the other. In this light, they are not healthy, they are discomforted; life is no longer worth living and this world will become inhabitable for them. Every human person is susceptible to this, because of the finitude of man.

After the fall of man, the world has become stressful for man. Take for instance: From the sweat shall man bring forth food and the woman shall labour in pain for child bearing"(See Genesis 3:16 -19). This was certainly not the situation in the past, but humanity cannot just continue in this way. This is why, from the benevolence of God Himself, He visited man greatly in the person of Jesus Christ, as He used to do with Adam and Eve in the Garden of Eden. So, God was the first to visit us.

---

[54] George W. Kosicki, *Demand Deeds of Mercy*, p. 34.

Jesus, who is our 'God-Man', continues to visit the human family in a particular sense. You recall the visit to the house of Lazarus and the nearby villages. When He was to depart physically from this world He said to the apostles: "Go ye to the whole world…" (Matthew 28:18). Thus, visitation includes necessarily the act of going: 'Going' here, would mean emptying oneself, so that we can be filled by Christ.

The natural inclination and desire for association places the imperative on men to visit one another. This will bring increase and refreshment. This visitation is not just to those who we know in order to have something or to beg for food or money, all in the name of visitation, and leave the needy behind. Whenever this is done, it is at best described as social work for entertainment but not work for love, charity and mercy. The visitation is to the needy hence, Jesus said, "When I was in the prison you visited me." Jesus has not given us any instruction without Himself doing the same first. The scripture records for instance, the visitation of Jesus and Peter to Peter's mother-in-law and Jesus calls us to do the same. Our sincere and genuine devotion to the work of visitation to the sick can be therapeutic. This can really bring healing to the sick through the instrumentality of the power of Jesus. By so doing, we become the channel through which divine grace is bestowed. As Christians, we are nothing other than the channel of Jesus' grace and blessing.

Although visitation necessarily requires going out of oneself, it is not only in the physical sense; it also requires us to be available when needed. Many are sick today, in addition to those in the hospital beds, who are living and doing the seemingly normal things, but they are diseased, disturbed, and not comfortable. Such people just need to identify, associate, speak to and share with others. Our availability, which can also be another form of visitation, is the medicine such people need. May we never deprive them of this opportunity.

5. Clothe the Naked

(Matthew 25:36; Isaiah 58:7; Ezekiel 18:7)

Nakedness is a greater sign of poverty. But beyond poverty, it is an exposure to attacks. For instance, if anyone is exposed to bad air and cold weather, the resultant effect is usually not palatable. Yet despite this knowledge, many people in our society today are still naked and we must give them clothes to wear.

Clothing is a basic element of human existence. Food and clothing are a blessing of God (read Deuteronomy 10:18; Genesis 2:8-9) ...since clothing is a protection against the inclemency of the weather, the poor man's cloak must not be kept in pawn when the nights' cold begins to descend on him (See Exodus 22:25). In addition to this rudimentary observation: the symbolism of clothing develops in two other dimensions: it is a sign of the definite order coming from the creator and likewise a symbol recalling the promise of a glory lost in paradise.[55]

Our Lord Jesus Christ was made to be naked during his passion (Matthew 27:35, John 19:23). Jesus then continues to identify with this people who are constantly ashamed of themselves. This is because of the passion inflicted on them, which has compulsorily stripped them naked. Their nakedness is not necessarily the absence of clothes; they have clothes to wear, but they are below standard. Some are tattered and have become unusable. Some people do not even have enough to take care of the bad ones they have. Jesus is easily found in the midst of such people.

Nakedness has become incompatible with human existence ever since the time of Adam and Eve. The author of the book of Genesis underscores this fact, that when the eyes of our first parents where opened, they got leaves to cover their body. Adam said to God that they hid themselves because they were naked (Genesis 3). Those who are naked in our world today, though full of potential that can be harnessed, are hiding. They are withdrawing themselves and cannot attain what Aristotle called *Entellenchi*. "How beautiful then is the ministry through

---

[55] Xavier Leon – Dufour, *Dictionary of Biblical Theology*, London: Burns and Oates, 1962, p. 81.

which we call forth and receive the hidden gifts of these people."[56]

When we clothe the naked, we keep them warm. By so doing, they will come out of themselves and will be able to actualize their potentiality rather than being limited by the coldness of this world. It is good, at this point, to note that clothing reveals the class to which one belongs in the society. Again, the word of Leon Xavier is helpful when he says: "clothing reflects the type of life lived in the social unit. For each part of the community acts as a harmonious life born of working together..."[57] Giving one's cloak is a sign of brotherhood. Jonathan sealed his covenant with David in this way (1 Sam 18:3ff), because clothing is intimately united with the person, a union evident to those who love the person..."[58]

Since God did not dismiss the sinner without clothing him, we who are the chosen ones of God, must continue in this work of God, who continues to clothe us. We must join Jesus Christ to restore the clothes of the possessed at Gerasenes (Mark 5:15). Each time we give clothes to the naked, we restore their hope, dignity, self-worth and self-possession like the father of the prodigal son did. We also restore the clothes of Jesus for which the soldiers cast lots during his passion. We, by so doing, remove the crown of thorns and restore the glory; for "in order that the glory of

---

[56] Henri J. M. Nouwen, *Clowning in Rome,* New York: Doubleday,1979.
[57] Xavier Leon-Dufour, *Dictionary of Biblical Theology,* pp. 82-83.
[58] Ibid.

Israel be adorned, Christ, the real servant, must be stripped of his clothing (Matthew 27:35, John 19: 23), be given up to a parody of kingly investiture (John 19: 3f), and become indistinguishably 'man', deprived of legal status."[59] But this man is the son of God whose glory is incorruptible.

Let me remind you of a story of Martin of Tours:

He was a roman soldier and a Christian. One cold winter day, as he was in a city, a beggar stopped him and asked for alms. Martin had no money; but the beggar was blue and shivering with cold, and Martin gave what he had. He took off his soldier's cloak. He cut it into two and gave half of it to the beggar man. That night, he had a dream. In it he saw the heavenly places and all the angels and Jesus among them. And Jesus was wearing half of a soldier's cloak. One of the angels said to him: "Master, why are you wearing that battered old cloak? Who gave it to you?" and Jesus answered softly: my servant Martin gave it to me.[60]

This is really a spiritual food for thought.

---

[59] Ibid.
[60] William Barclay, *The Gospel of Matthew, Volume 2*, p. 381.

6. Habour the Homeless

(Matthew 25:35; Hebrews 13:2)

"We must not forget that we are pilgrims journeying alongside one another."[61] Another demand of the works of mercy is the requirement to harbour the homeless. Another version of the Christian Scriptures may present it as - shelter the stranger. This latter part captures the idea very well, that is, to shelter the stranger. "A stranger is a person that you do not know."[62] Also, a stranger is a person who is new to an environment and who has not yet acquired domicile in any form in such an environment. Such a person is practically in need of help. Such a person need not only a house, but also a home. There is a need for a home for them to be balanced and to actualize fully their human personality and potentiality. One becomes a stranger because one is not born in a place. Some have become strangers because of the evils of war and hunger. For instance, the internally displaced presence in many parts of Africa and refugees looking for asylum all over the world. This can happen to anyone. That is to say that anybody can become a stranger.

The present Pontiff, Francis, reminds us: "We must never forget that we are pilgrims journeying alongside one

---

[61] Pope Francis, *Evangelism Gaudium, no. 244.*
[62] *Oxford Advanced Learners Dictionary*, 6th Edition, Sallywelmeier (ed), Oxford: Oxford University Press, 2000, S.V. "Strangers".

another."[63] The fact that we are in our abode does not mean that we cannot be strangers. In fact, we are naturally strangers because we are sojourners in this world. It is quite difficult anyway to accommodate the persons we do not know in this present time because of the mistrust that is present almost everywhere. This mistrust might have arisen from the level of insecurity in many countries. But Pope Francis exhorts us again: "This means that we must have sincere trust in our fellow pilgrims, putting aside all suspicion or mistrust, and turn our face to what we are all seeking, the radiant peace of God's face."[64]

There may be separation because of the boundaries set by men, but there is at least one thing that binds us together. Christians are bound together by the reception of the Sacrament of Baptism. The Catholic leaders have this to say: "the fullness of catholicity proper to her in those her children who, though joined to her by Baptism, are yet separated from full communion with her."[65] The Pope continued to say: "How many important things unite us! If we really believe in the abundantly free working of the Holy Spirit, we can learn so much from one another."[66] Indeed, we have so much to learn and gain from the strangers we welcome and take care of like the widow of Zarephath, who welcomed the prophet Elijah.

---

[63] Pope Francis, *Evangelium Gaudium*, no. 244.
[64] Ibid.
[65] Second Vatican Council, *Decree on Ecumenism, Unitatis Redintegratio*, no. 4.
[66] Pope Francis, *Evangelii Gaudium*, no. 246.

We are all called to this vocation.

At a number of points, Christian positions permit and encourage collaboration with other spiritual and ideological families. Therefore, councils and ecumenical organizations rightly pay attention to possible areas of collaboration, e.g., housing.[67]

Each time we give housing and shelter to those who need it, we take the baby Jesus out of the manger and put Him in our well designed and decent houses. He, in turn, will then be dwelling as the king of our homes and ordain peace for us. May we never deny housing and shelter to those who need it. (Amen).

7. Comfort the Prisoner

(Matthew 25:36; Luke 4:18ff)

"Untie him", Jesus told them, "and let him go" (John 11:44) Prison is "a building or other facility used for holding individuals in judicial confinement."[68] Prison experiences are usually not comfortable and pleasing to the one passing through the experience. In those days, many

---

[67] Ecumenical Collaboration at the Regional, National and Local levels, 1975, in Austin Flannery (ed), Collection volume 2 (Vatican council II), More Post Vatican Conciliar Documents, Mumbai: St. Pauls, 1982, p. 198.
[68] Harper Collins, *Bible Dictionary*, Paul J. Achtemier Bangalore: Theological publications in India, 2009, p. 88.

prisoners were in chains even until this time, the experience is still remembered.

Many states today are making frantic efforts to build more prisons. But is this to bring comfort to the inmates? Certainly not. It is simply to decongest the existing yards and to avoid prison breaks. There is much more to be done than building more prison yards. We must also bring comfort to those in prison.

The first reason is because the inmates could be any one of us. Really, there are many prisoners today who are innocent, many of whom are awaiting trial. Again, Jesus is always with them. Thus, He says: "When I was imprisoned, you visited me" (Matthew 25). Indeed, Jesus is always in prison. The experience of Jesus' Apostles in prison is a clear evidence that Jesus is with His people even in prison.

Our visitation to the prison can be a means of taking the goodness of Christ to the poor. Our visitation to the prison helps us to participate in the execution of Jesus' manifesto when He says: "The spirit of the Lord is upon me…to proclaim freedom to the captives" (Luke 4:18ff).

In those days, to be in prison was not necessarily for punishment in itself; it was rather, a detention for trial. Joseph of course was the first prisoner mentioned in the Old Testament of the Christian Scriptures (Genesis 39:20). Also, prophets who had made themselves enemies of the rulers of their time were also imprisoned. Jeremiah (Jeremiah 32:2, 37:21) is a good example of this.[69]

We must also take note that there are many things that imprison human beings today. In fact, our world has almost become a huge prison yard. We are not free even in our homes. This is quite evident in the kind of fences we now use today and the iron doors in our homes. Jean Jacque Rousseau understands this clearly and says that man is free but everywhere in chains.[70]

All of us are therefore called to free ourselves from the shackles of sin and other things that constantly put us in captivity. By visiting the imprisoned, we may also be free from their psychological bondage.

Conclusion

Finally, at this juncture, I would like to leave you all with the following words of our dear Archbishop Fulton Sheen:

By thinking of others we get God to think of us. Mercy is a compassion that seeks to unburden the sorrows of others as if they were our own. But if

---

[69] Scott Hahn (E. d.), *Catholic Bible Dictionary*, New York: Doubleday, 2009, p. 730.
[70] Jean Jacque Rousseau, *The Social Contract or Principles of Political Right*, Transl. by Henry J. Tozer, London: Swan Sonnenschein & Co, 1895.

we show no such compassion, then how can compassion ever come back to us? Unless we throw something up, nothing will come down; unless there is action, there can never be a reaction, unless we give, it shall not be given to us.[71]

We should also keep in mind the words of Tobit: "Almsgiving delivers from death and it will purge away every sin" (Tobit 12:9). Let us make constant and conscious effort to feed the hungry, give water to the thirsty, visit the sick and the imprisoned, shelter the homeless, clothe the naked and bury the dead. For in this we manifest God's mercy to the whole world and through them we find the Lord and serve Him. May He crown our efforts of showing mercy to others, especially the under-privileged and the needy in our society, with success.

When we engage in spiritual and corporal works of mercy, we become beautiful fragments of light in a dark and decaying world. We radiate God's love and mercy and thus become the visible manifestation of God's Divine Mercy for all sinners in the world. The next chapter will talk about the need for reconciliation with God and neighbour as every one of our attempts to keep up with our works of mercy leads us steadily to an intimacy with God and our neighbour. There is the need therefore, to constantly renew our relationship with God and return to Him when we fall.

---

[71] Fulton J. Sheen, *The Cross and the Beatitudes (Lessons on Love and Forgiveness)*, Liguori: Liguori Publications, 2000, p. 31.

This also necessitates that we are at peace with our neighbour.

Above all, we must learn from Our Lady, Mother of mercy, whose heart the Curé of Ars described thus: "The heart of this good Mother is all love and mercy; she desires only to see us happy. We have only to turn to her and be heard... in that of the most holy Virgin, there is nothing but mercy."[72]

---

[72] St. John Vianney, *Little Catechism of the Cure of Ars*, p. 14.

CHAPTER FOUR

THE NEED FOR RECONCILIATION WITH GOD AND NEIGHBOUR IN THE LIGHT OF THE EXTRA ORDINARY JUBILEE YEAR OF MERCY

Introduction

Spiritual meditation is an integral part of our Christian life. A Christian life without a periodic and thorough examination is not worth living. As the popular Greek philosopher, Socrates, once put it: "An unexamined life is not worth living." Periods of daily examination, monthly recollection, and annual retreats are necessary for a closer and deeper look into the meaning and purpose of life. It is a search into a higher and greater purpose of life. It is a way of having access to inner solace and a flashback on life in the past, the nature of life presently in order to know the way forward for a better life in the future. It is an authentic way of accessing your true self either positively or negatively. This could be done at the level of the individual, which is generally referred to as self - evaluation. It could be moderated by a spiritual director or a person so chosen by the group, which is referred to as directed recollection.

During recollection, we ask questions like: Who am I? Where am I? Why am I here on earth? What is the meaning of life? How can I attain inner peace? Where was I? Where am I now? It is also pertinent for us to consider our relationship with those around us. What is the relationship between me and my family members, my parishioners, and those placed under my care? (to mention but a few) You have spent this number of months/years in life. It is wholesome and befitting to access the journey so far and how it has influenced your life and the life of others, to strive towards holiness of life and salvation. How will your life and ministry so far influence your life and those of others in the future? Bear in mind that a recollection demands a degree of silence and a sober reflection for it to be worthy of the time and sacrifice made to experience it. It is this sober reflection that will further bring about the need to reconcile with one another and seek the mercy of God. According to the Holy Father, Pope Francis, in his Bull of Indiction of the Extraordinary Jubilee Year of Mercy, "I ask that the season of Lent in this Jubilee year be lived more intensely as a privileged moment to celebrate and experience God's mercy."[73] The efficacy of God's mercy can only be complete when it is celebrated both at the horizontal (with fellow human beings) and vertical levels (with God). This is the reason why the theme for this part of our reflection is: "The Need for Reconciliation with God in Light of the Extraordinary Jubilee Year of Mercy."

---

[73] Pope Francis, *Misericordiae Vultus,* no. 17.

This part examines the need for reconciliation with God, the Church, and among God's people in order to bring about peace, unity and unending progress within the individual, the particular and universal Church, to make the Church holy and salvific in her mission.

What is Reconciliation?

Reconciliation in the sense we are using it, is the restoration of friendly relationships. It is also an act of reconciling or the state of being reconciled.[74] Imagine two friends who have a fight or argument, the good relationship they once enjoyed is strained to the point of breaking. They cease speaking to each other; communication is deemed too awkward. The friends gradually become strangers. Such estrangement can only be reversed by reconciliation. To be reconciled is to be restored to friendship or harmony. When old friends resolve their differences and restore their relationship, reconciliation has occurred. 2 Corinthians 5:18-19 declares:

> All this is from God, who reconciled us to himself through Christ and gave us the ministry of reconciliation: that God was reconciling the world to himself in Christ, not counting men's sins

---

[74] Random House Webster's Unabridged Dictionary, Robert B. Costello, et al, (ed). New York: Random house publishers, U.S.A, 2001, p. 1612.

against them. And he has committed to us the message of reconciliation.

The Bible says that Christ reconciled us to God (Romans 5:10; 2 Corinthians 5:18; Colossians 1:20-21). The fact that we needed reconciliation means that our relationship with God was broken. Since God is holy, we were the ones to blame. Our sins alienated us from Him. Romans 5:10 says that we were enemies of God: "Once enemies of God, we were reconciled to him through the death of his Son, how much more, having been reconciled, shall we be saved through his life!"

For Pope Benedict XVI: "We are invited to be reconciled with our inner selves, to become joyful instruments of Divine Mercy, each of us contributing our own spiritual and material riches to the common commitment."[75] When Christ died on the cross, He satisfied God's judgment and made it possible for God's enemies, (us), to find peace with Him. Our "reconciliation" to God, then, involves the exercise of His grace and the forgiveness of our sins. The result of Jesus' sacrifice is that our relationship has changed from enmity to friendship. "I no longer call you servants ... Instead, I have called you friends" (John 15:15). Christian reconciliation is a glorious truth! We were God's enemies but are now His friends. We were in a state of condemnation because of our sins, but we

---

[75] Ron Gagne, http://www.lasalette.org/reflections/632-pope-benedict-on-reconciliation-in-africa.html, accessed on March 7, 2016.

are now forgiven. We were at war with God, but now have the peace that transcends all understanding (Philippians 4:7). According to His Holiness, Pope Francis:

> Through the Sacrament of Reconciliation, which flows from the Paschal Mystery, the forgiveness we receive is not the result of our own efforts but is the gift of the Holy Spirit reconciling us to God and to each other. .... The Sacrament of Reconciliation calls us back to God and embraces us with his infinite mercy and joy. May we allow his love to renew us as his children and to reconcile us with him, with ourselves, and with one another.[76]

Reconciliation with God

Reconciliation with God is the most important aspect of reconciliation because of the primacy of God in the scheme of Divine Mercy. This can be found fully in the Sacrament of Reconciliation. Jesus knew very well that after His physical departure from this world, His disciples and would-be followers were going to stray from the right path. So, for them to reconcile with God, He decided to

---

[76] Pope Francis: Catechesis on the Sacrament of Reconciliation, at the Vatican Radio on the 19th Feb. 2014.

institute the Sacrament of Penance: This is regarded as complete when one goes through the tripartite process of contrition, confession and satisfaction. The mercy of God for repentant sinners is depicted and exemplified by many parables in the Bible like: the parable of the prodigal son, the dutiful son and the merciful father (Luke 15:11-31), the story of the adulterous woman (John 8:1-13), the parable of the wicked servant (Matthew 18:23-35), to mention but a few. These parables all show that our God is a merciful Father who is always ready to forgive the offences and faults of all His children who have sinned against Him. As people of God we are called to be conscious always of this basic fact: that our God is a merciful father and that we should teach our lay faithful to be aware of this basic reality. The only way to peace and mutual togetherness is reconciliation. Christ is our peace and reconciliation. It is through our righteous and holy union and fellowship with God that we find our true peace. (See Matthew 5:23-24; 18:15-20.)

It is imperative that we endeavour to go to Confession and encourage others to do same especially during this season of Lent, which for me is the heart of the Extraordinary Jubilee Year of Mercy for all of Christ's faithful all over the world. These parables, however, certainly mirror our situation, both in our vertical relationship with God and our horizontal relationship with our fellow men and women. They not only illustrate the imperative to ask for forgiveness, but they also offer reasons why we should forgive others.[77] Having reconciled with God, we owe it as a duty to God, to the Church and to our fellow brothers and sisters to reconcile with one another. This brings us to the next level of reconciliation which is reconciliation among ourselves as individuals and members of the same family of God's people.

Reconciliation with our Neighbour

This is the second level of reconciliation and it is this level that makes reconciliation to be complete and wholesome. It gives integrity and credibility to the whole idea of reconciliation and forgiveness of sin. The Bible, through the parable of the Good Samaritan (Luke10:25-37), already showed vividly to us who our neighbour is. Any human person, irrespective of age, position, class, colour, race, tribe and sex, created in the image and likeness of God, is your neighbour. No matter what anybody might have done to us as children of the Most High God, be they clergy, religious and lay faithful, the horizontal dimension of reconciliation calls and invites us to forgive and reconcile with those who may have offended us. One of the lessons of the parable of the unforgiving and wicked servant is that, if God is merciful enough to forgive us our trespasses, we

---

[77] Cf. Damian Ilodigwe, *Faith in Action*, Ibadan: St Paul's Publications, 2014, p. 173.

should be merciful enough to forgive others. Jesus said, "That is how my heavenly Father will deal with you unless you each forgive your brother from your heart" (Matthew 18:35), just like the unforgiving servant. "Yes, if you forgive others their failings, your heavenly Father will forgive you yours; but if you do not forgive others, your heavenly Father will not forgive you" (Matthew 6:14-15). This is one of the signs of love for God and neighbour. "Anyone who says 'I love God' and hates his brother is a liar, since whoever does not love the brother whom he can see cannot love God whom he cannot see" (1John 4:20). Love does not take offence or store up grievances. (1Corinthians 13:5)

What if the person offended us many times? What are we expected to do? You recall that Peter said to Jesus, how many times must I forgive my brother if he wrongs me, as often as seven times? Jesus answered, not seven, I tell you but seventy-seven times (Matthew 18:21-22). You will agree with me that it will be difficult for someone to offend you such a number of times. What the Lord is simply telling us is that we should forgive as many times as anybody offends us. In other words, there is no limit to forgiveness and reconciliation (Cf. Luke17:4). We are therefore obliged to forgive not only when we want to, but we must forgive as often as we are offended. Unless we forgive as often as we are offended, we may not expect to receive forgiveness from God. In answering Peter's question, this is the message which Jesus delivers unequivocally to Peter and all of us. As human beings, we are expected to proclaim this message loud and clearer than before, to all people, in season and out of season.

In Luke 17:4, Jesus said, "If he wronged you seven times a day and seven times comes back to you and says, 'I am sorry,' you must forgive him." The question that readily comes to mind at this juncture is, what if the one who wrongs you does not come back to you to say I am sorry, what do you do? Jesus knew that there were going to be cases of this nature, that was why He said in the Gospel of Matthew 18:15-17, "If your brother does something wrong, go and have it out with him alone, between yourselves. ...If he does not listen, take one or two others along with you. ...But if he refuses to listen to these, report it to the community, and if he refuses to listen to the community, treat him like a gentile or a tax collector", so that the work of conversion may begin.

For some people treating him like a gentile or a tax collector is like saying: go your way and make the person an enemy. Leave the person alone and live your life. The other question that readily comes to mind is: How did Jesus Christ treat gentiles and tax collectors? The example of the faith of the Canaanite woman, who was herself a gentile, which made her daughter to be healed by Jesus (Matt.15:21-28), and the rescue efforts of the good Samaritan who saved the life of the man who was attacked by brigands on his way from Jerusalem to Jericho (Cf. Luke 10:25-37), are clear cut examples of the relationship that existed between Jesus and the gentiles. Although he knew that they were discriminated against by the Jews, His own people, He had a cordial relationship with them and related with them well. As for tax collectors, the call of Matthew illustrates the way Jesus related with tax collectors. It was even while He was eating with tax collectors, who were called sinners and discriminated against, that He called Matthew to be his disciple. It is obvious and apparent that Jesus related well with tax collectors and gentiles. So, the implication of treating the person as a tax collector or gentile is that you continue to treat such difficult and unrepentant people with continuous love, care and affection, maintaining the relationship until such a time that the person will realize the reason to reconcile with you or with those who may have offended him or her.

In our reconciliation with God and our fellow human beings, there should be no barrier. There should be no reason why you cannot reconcile with your brother or your sister. The Lord Jesus showed this in the Scriptures in so many ways as demonstrated above. Love is patient and as such we should be patient in reconciling and forgiving one another as God is always and consistently patient and kind with us in forgiving whenever we offend Him. This is one of the attributes of God as shown in the fig tree that did not bear fruit (Luke 13:6f). The Lord is always giving us time to repent and change from our evil ways and come back to Him.

Feelings and emotions about offences and sins committed should not be an obstacle to forgiveness.

Human beings like us should not be obstacles to our readiness to forgive offences against us. Even Jesus, while on the cross of Calvary, forgave those who crucified Him before He died. The clergy among the people of God has an obligation in fact, as dispensers of the mysteries of salvation, to be detached while forgiving and reconciling the people with God. They have an obligation to proclaim and teach the people in their various places of apostolate. They should also be available to organize confessions and penitential services to ensure that the people of God are able to avail themselves of these opportunities.

In doing this, the authority and the theology behind the forgiveness of sin should be occasionally explained and taught so that the people will not lose sight of the efficacy of this Sacrament in their life and in the life of the Church.

Reconciliation within the Context of the Extraordinary Jubilee Year of Mercy

There are always vertical and horizontal consequences for sin (be it reserved or not). At the vertical level, it severs our relationship with God, while at the horizontal level, it affects our relationship with one another and with the

Church. "It creates a rupture between us and the Church."[78] Sin creates a barrier between us and the Church, the community of God's people. No matter how intimate or secret a sin is, there is a social dimension to it.[79] It is in such a manner that it affects the holiness and the unity that should exist in the Church as the body of Christ here on earth.

Usually, within the context of reconciliation in the Church, there is this whole idea of reserved sin. Reserved sin is meant to fulfill the twofold aim of healing us from our sins and bringing us to reconciliation with God and His Church. "This is because it is one thing to be healed, and it is something else to be fully reconciled after healing. Reconciliation involves reparation. In this way mercy does not annul but helps to fulfill the demands of Justice."[80]

The penance we are given after confession attests to the presence of a debt to pay for complete reconciliation. That penance is called satisfaction, which is the last process of the Sacrament of Reconciliation. Although satisfaction is not a condition for forgiveness, it is, however, part of the process of reconciliation. The practice of indulgence comes

---

[78] Idahosa Amadasu, "The meaning of Reserved Sins," A Paper presented at the Study session with the Formators at the Seminary of All Saints, Uhiele, Ekpoma, on February 16, 2016 p. 2.
[79] Pope John Paul II, Post Synodal Apostolic Exhortation, *Reconciliation and Peace*, http://w2vatican.va/content/johnpauli/en/apost_exhortations/documents/hf_jpii_exh_02121984_reconcilatio-paenitentia.html16, Accessed on March 6, 2016.
[80] Ibid.

from the possibility that we may not completely make satisfaction for our sins or that there may be some minor sins that need to be remitted. Indulgence is the Church's way of making God's mercy more accessible to us whether we are living or dead.[81] Theologically and Canonically for the sake of clarity, we speak of remission of reserved penalties rather than reserved sins. This is because if one is sorry for sin, no human power can deny the person's forgiveness. (Cf. canon 1358)

So, what really remains or is reserved after confession is the punishment due to forgiven sin. So, after healing from sin through forgiveness, there is need to reconcile with the Church. The gravity of some of these sins makes the Church to clearly stipulate their penalty. Those penalties that are incurred by the very fact of the sin are called *latae sententiae*, a Latin phrase meaning 'sentence already passed.' It is by the very fact of committing the act that one incurs the penalty, which is usually excommunication. That is, one is no longer in communion with the Church or an interdict, which is the same as suspension from certain Church practices or functions. There is another type of penalty called *ferendae sententiae,* meaning 'sentence to be passed' when declared or imposed. *Latae sententiae* applies even when this has not been declared or made public. Some of these penalties are established by the Roman Pontiff or any of the Roman Dicastries competent to do so. These

---

[81] Ibid.

penalties are universal and only the Holy See or its delegated authority can remit the punishment.

There are other kinds of penalties that are established by the Episcopal Conferences, provincial councils and diocesan bishops. These are called particular (c. 1315).

The censures or penalty that can be remitted only by the Holy See are:

- The desecration of the Sacred Species (c. 1367),
- Violence against the Roman Pontiff (c. 1370),
- Attempted absolution of a partner in sin against the sixth commandment of the Decalogue (c. 1378),
- Direct violation of the seal of confession (c. 1388),
- Consecration of a bishop without pontifical mandate (c. 1382), and
- A priest who assists in the completion of an abortion (cc.1041, n. 4, §1, n.3).

Penalties not reserved to the Holy See but which a diocesan bishop may reserve the faculty to remit to himself or his delegates are:

- *Latae sententiae* interdict for lay person and *latae sententiae* suspension for priests who use physical force against the bishop (c. 1370, § 2),
- *Latae sententiae* of completed abortion (1398),

- And penalty for heresy, apostasy, and schism. Canon 751 defines these three acts thus:

Heresy is the obstinate post-baptismal denial of some truth which must be believed with divine and catholic faith, or it is likewise an obstinate doubt concerning same; apostasy is the total repudiation of the Christian faith; schism is the refusal of submission to the Roman Pontiff or of communion with the members of the church subject to him.[82]

Hitherto, the above-mentioned penalties or censures were in vogue in the Church. The dawn of the Extraordinary Jubilee Year of Mercy saw the emergence of two significant offers from the Holy Father, Pope Francis. The first is the broadening of the faculty to remit the penalty due to the reserved sin of abortion to all priests, which is ordinarily under the competence of bishops or those so delegated by them. The second is the sending out of the Apostles and Missionaries of Mercy to remit the reserved sins proper to the Holy See.[83] Even after the Extraordinary

---

[82] Cf. Idahosa Amadasu, "The Meaning of Reserved Sins". 4.

[83] Pope Francis, "letter on the granting of indulgence to the faithful on the occasion of the Extraordinary Jubilee Year of Mercy" http://w2.vatican.va/content/francesco/en/letters/2015/documents/papa -francesco_20150901_lettera-indulgenza-giubileo-misericodia.html. ,accessed on March 6, 2016. Pope Francis *Misericordai Vultus*, Bull of Indiction of the Extraordinary Jubilee Year of Mercy, April 11, 2015. Kenya: Pauline's Publications Africa, 18.

Jubilee Year of Mercy, the faculty to remit the penalty due to the reserved sin of abortion is still given to all priests; so is the mandate given to the Missionaries of Mercy.

Conclusion

Based on our assessment so far, the need for reconciliation with one another, the Church and God cannot be overemphasized every moment of our lives as Christians. God has shown vividly, through the parables earlier cited in this book, that He is a merciful and forgiving Father. He has shown to us and has called us to avail ourselves of this year of mercy to ask for forgiveness of our sins. As we reconcile with God, we must continually be conscious that the fullness of reconciliation can only be realized, not just by going to Confession and asking God for forgiveness through the Church, but also in our reconciliation with one another. There should be no reason why we should not reconcile with one another. This, Christ has shown in our reflection on the reconciliation with our neighbour.

Finally, the Jubilee Year of Mercy, celebrated in the year 2015, is an ample reminder of the need for us to exemplify the mercy of God among ourselves as we have been exhorted on the need to avail ourselves of the privileges provided by this Year of Mercy. This is unique, especially regarding the reserved sin of abortion, which could be absolved by all priests during this year of mercy. It is gratifying to know that the Holy Father has extended the work of the Apostles of Mercy and the Missionaries of Mercy during the Year till further notice. It shows that there is no limit to Divine Mercy. As a people of God, we should also use the extension of the commissioning and mandate given by the Holy Father, Pope Francis, to Apostles of Mercy and Missionaries of Mercy to reconcile with God and the Church - the Body of Christ here on earth[84] so that the Church Universal will truly and fully reconcile herself with God, our merciful Father. It is only a true and authentic reconciliation with one another and with God that can bring about inner peace, profound unity and a robust progress in different parishes, ecclesial institutions, dioceses and the Universal Church in general.

May our Mother Mary, Mother of Mercy, intercede for us as we reconcile with one another, with the Church and with God, the merciful Father through Christ our Lord. Amen.

---

[84] The reserved sins are as follows: 1. Profaning the Eucharistic species by taking them away or keeping them for sacrilegious purpose 2. Use of physical force against the Roman Pontiff 3. Absolution of an accomplice in a sin against the sixth commandment of the Decalogue 4. A direct violation against the sacramental seal by confessor.

FINAL THOUGHTS

We began with an introduction on why we are writing this book, which is meant to help us as members of Christ's faithful to be in union with the Holy Mother Church. We recall that the Church celebrated the Extraordinary Jubilee Year of Mercy, which began on December 8th, 2015, as was announced by Pope Francis on Divine Mercy Sunday, the 13th of April 2015. Secondly, it will afford us, Christ's faithful, the opportunity to see how we can readily make more meaningful the mercy of God in our daily lives and the lives of all in the world today.

Our assessment began with the idea of Divine Mercy in the Bible (Old and New Testaments). It is obvious from our study that the Old and New Testaments are united in their affirmation that the God of the Bible is a merciful and compassionate God. The Fathers of the Church attested and witnessed to this affirmation

We dwelt in detail on the spiritual and corporal works of mercy. Our study of Divine Mercy from these different perspectives led to examination of the need for mercy and recollection among Christians today, using the Sacrament of Reconciliation as a veritable means of reconciling with God and His faithful people here on earth - The Church. We also identified the centrality of the spiritual works of mercy and the corporal works of mercy. The Lenten season, during the Year of Mercy, provided ample opportunity for the faithful to reconcile with one another and with God. It was also an opportunity to gain indulgences, with the role of our Blessed Mother Mary, refuge of sinners, as our maternal intercessor re-emphasized.

In the same chapter, we looked at a few of the Church's Fathers' perspectives, especially the three most recent Popes in the history of the Church. We reviewed the Bull of Indiction, *Misericordiae Vultus,* released by Pope Francis, by articulating the major themes of the different sections and their relevance to the general theme of the celebration of the Extraordinary Jubilee Year of Mercy, which is entitled, *Merciful like the Father.*

The third chapter examined the spiritual works of mercy, namely: counselling the doubtful, admonishing the sinner, instructing the ignorant, comforting the sorrowful, bearing wrongs patiently, forgiving injuries and praying for the living and the dead. The fourth chapter is on the corporal works of mercy, viz: feed the hungry, give water to the thirsty, bury the dead, visit the sick, clothe the naked, harbour the homeless and comfort the prisoner. We were all encouraged to practice these works of mercy.

In all but one of the cases, failure to perform the spiritual and corporal works of mercy constitutes a sin of omission. Failure to forgive injuries becomes a sin of commission, which is why we studied the need for reconciliation with God within and outside the context of the Year of Mercy today.

It is part of our Christian calling to endeavor to go and put into practice what we have studied and make good use of the fruits of the Year of Mercy. The study of this book provides ample opportunities to be more enlightened and inspired to be merciful through our spiritual commitments to reconciliation between God and our fellow human beings. The practice of the spiritual and corporal works of mercy will enable us to gain indulgences and graces, so that, as Christians, we may consistently be in communion with God, the Church and one another in the most holy way and in our general attitude towards life.

SELECTED BIBLIOGRAPHY

Books

AQUINAS, Thomas, Summa Theologica, London: Catholic Way Publishing, 2014.

BARCLAY, William, *The New Daily Study Bible, the Gospel of Matthew,* Bangalore: Theological Publications India, 2009.

DUFOUR, Xavier Leon, *Dictionary of Biblical Theology*, London: Burns and Oates, 1962.

GANDHI, Mahatma, *Gandhi on Non-Violence*, New York: New Directions Publishing, 2007.

GRIZEZ, Germain, *The May of the Lord Jesus: Difficult Moral questions,* Illinois: Franciscan Press, 1997.

HAHN, Scott (E. d.), *Catholic Bible Dictionary*, New York: Doubleday, 2009.

IKEKE, Mark O., *Race and Racism (a Socio-Political and Philosophic Anthropology,* Awka, Nigeria: Fab Educational Books, 2011.

ILODIGWE, Damian, *Faith in Action*, Ibadan: St Paul's Publications, 2014.

IROEGBU, Pantaleon, *Kpim of Time: Eternity*, Ibadan: Hope Publications, 2004.

KAITHOLIL, George, *Mercy; Divine and Human,* Mumbai: St. Pauls Publications, 2015.

KOSICKI, George W. *I Demand Deeds of Mercy,* Mumbai: St. Pauls Publications, 2000.

LAWHEAD, William, *The Voyage of Discovery,* Ohio: Wadsworth, 2002.

HEIDEGGER, Martin, *Being and Time* transl. by Translated by John Macquarrie & Edward Robinson London: S.C.M. Press, 1962.

MCBRIEN, Richard, *Catholicism,* New York: Harper San Francisco, 1994.

NOUWEN, Henri J. M., *Clowning in Rome,* New York: Doubleday, 1979.

PERRIN, J. M., "Works of Mercy" in *New Catholic Encyclopedia,* vol. ix. Washington DC: Jack Heraty and Associates Inc., 1967.

RAHNER, Karl (ed.), *Encyclopedia of Theology.* London: Burns and Oates, 1975.

RICCIO, Dolores, *Supper Food for Women,* New York: Warner Books, 1996.

ROUSSEAU, Jean Jacque, *The Social Contract or Principles of Political Right,* Transl. by Henry J. Tozer, London: Swan Sonnenschein & Co, 1895.

SHEEN, Fulton J., *The Cross and the Beatitudes (Lessons on Love Forgiveness)*, Liguori: Liguori Publications, 2000

St. Augustine, *The Christian Life*, compiled by Anthony Tonna-Barthet, J.F McGowan (trans.), New York: Frederich Pustet Co. (Inc) 1929.

Articles

AMADASU, Idahosa, "The meaning of Reserved Sins," A Paper presented at the Study session with the Formators at the Seminary of All Saints, Uhiele, Ekpoma, on February 16, 2016.

Ecumenical Collaboration at the Regional, National and Local levels, 1975, in Austin Flannery (ed), Collection volume 2 (Vatican council II), More Post Vatican Conciliar Documents, Mumbai: St. Pauls Publications, 1982.

OGBUNWUEZEH, Emmanuel Franklyne, "Death in Igbo Conceptual Schemes - a Therapy of myth, Mystery and Metaphysics" in *The Kpim of Death Essays in Memory of Rev. Fr. Prof. Panteleon Ireogbu*, George Uzoma (ed), Bloomington: Trafford Publishing, 2007.

Church Documents

Dives in Misericordia (Rich in Mercy), The Encyclical letter of Pope John Paul II, 30th November 1980.

Laudato Si, Apostolic Exhortation of Pope Francis on Care for our Common Home.

Sacramentum Caritatis, Benedict XVI, *The Holy Eucharist, the Sacrament of Charity.*

Mater et Magistra, Encyclical Letter of Pope John XXIII, 1961.

Evangelii Gaudium, Encyclical Letter of Pope Francis on the Joy of the Gospel.

Second Vatican Council, *Decree on Ecumenism, Unitatis Redintegratio.*

Misericordia Vultus, Pope Francis Bull of Indiction of the Extraordinary Jubilee Year of Mercy.

Pacem in Terris, Pope John Paul II, Post Synodal Apostolic Exhortation on *Reconciliation and Peace.*

Internet Sources

http://www.usccb.org/beliefs-and-teachings/how-we-teach/new-evangelization/jubilee-of-mercy/the-spiritual-works-of-mercy.cfm, accessed on May 16, 2016.

http://www.unfoundation.org/blog/12-nelson-mandela-quotes.html, accessed on August 28, 2018.

Ron Gagne, http://www.lasalette.org/reflections/632-pope-benedict-on-reconciliation-in-africa.html, accessed on March 7, 2016.

http//w2vatican.va/content/johnpauli/en/apost_exhortations/documents/hf_jpii_exh_02121984_reconcilatio-paenitentia.html16, accessed on March 6, 2016.

Pope Francis, "Letter on the granting of indulgence to the faithful on the occasion of the Extraordinary Jubilee Year of Mercy", http://w2.vatican.va/content/francesco/en/letters/2015/documents/papa-francesco_20150901_lettera-indulgenza-giubileo-misericodia.html, accessed on March 6, 2016.

Other Materials

Conferencia Nacional Dos Bispos Do Brazil, Ezigencias Evangelicans e Eticas De Superecao Miseria E da Fome, 2002, no. 2.

HANDELSMAN, Jacob C. (ed.), *The Concise Medical Encyclopedia,* , New York: Ottenheimer Pub Co, 1998.

Harper Collins, Bible Dictionary, Paul J. Achtemier Bangalore: Theological Publications in India, 2009.

HUNTER, Rodney J., *Dictionary of Pastoral Care and Counselling,* Nashville: Abingdon Press, 1990.

Oxford Advanced Learners Dictionary, 6th Edition, A. S. Hornby (Author) Sally Wehmeier (ed), Oxford: Oxford University Press, 2000.

Pope Francis: Catechesis on the Sacrament of Reconciliation, at the Vatican Radio on the 19th Feb. 2014.

Random House Webster's Unabridged Dictionary, Robert B. Costello, et al, (ed). New York: Random House Publishers, 2001.

St. John Vianney, *Little Catechism of the Cure of Ars*, Charlotte: TAN Books, 1994.

United States Catechism for Adults, Washington, DC: United States Conference of Catholic Bishops, 2006.

www.ingramcontent.com/pod-product-compliance
Lightning Source LLC
LaVergne TN
LVHW051657080426
835511LV00017B/2615